The LOCUS Distributed System Architecture

MIT Press Series in Computer Systems
Herb Schwetman, editor

Metamodeling: A Study of Approximations in Queueing Models, by Subhash Chandra Agrawal, 1985

Logic Testing and Design for Testability, by Hideo Fujiwara, 1985

Performance and Evaluation of Lisp Systems, by Richard P. Gabriel, 1985

The LOCUS Distributed System Architecture, edited by Gerald Popek and Bruce J. Walker, 1985

The LOCUS Distributed System Architecture

edited by
Gerald J. Popek and Bruce J. Walker

The MIT Press
Cambridge, Massachusetts
London, England

Publisher's note: This format is intended to reduce the cost of publishing certain works in book form and to shorten the gap between editorial preparation and final publication. Detailed editing and composition have been avoided by photographing the text of this book directly from the author's typescript or word-processor output.

Library of Congress Cataloging-in-Publication Data
Main entry under title:

The LOCUS distributed system architecture.

(MIT Press series in computer systems)
Bibliography: p.
Includes index.
1. LOCUS (Computer operating system) 2. Computer
architecture. 3. Electronic data processing—Distributed
processing. I. Popek, Gerald. II. Walker, Bruce J.
III. Series.
QA76.76.063L63 1985   005.4'3   85-18157
ISBN 978-0-262-16102-2 (hc. : alk. paper)—978-0-262-51719-5 (pb. : alk. paper)

To all the families and relationships which endured

Contents

Figures

Series Foreword

This series is devoted to all aspects of computer systems. This means that subjects ranging from circuit components and microprocessors to architecture to supercomputers and systems programming will be appropriate. Analysis of systems will be important as well. System theories are developing, theories that permit deeper understandings of complex interrelationships and their effects on performance, reliability, and usefulness.

We expect to offer books that not only develop new material but also describe projects and systems. In addition to understanding concepts, we need to benefit from the decision making that goes into actual development projects; selection from various alternatives can be crucial to success. We are soliciting contributions in which several aspects of systems are classified and compared. A better understanding of both the similarities and the differences found in systems is needed.

It is an exciting time in the area of computer systems. New technologies mean that architectures that were at one time interesting but not feasible are now feasible. Better software engineering means that we can consider several software alternatives, instead of "more of the same old thing," in terms of operating systems and system software. Faster and cheaper communications mean that intercomponent distances are less important. We hope that this series contributes to this excitement in the area of computer systems by chronicling past achievements and publicizing new concepts. The format allows publication of lengthy presentations that are of interest to a select readership.

Herb Schwetman

Preface

Distributed, interconnected and cooperating computing systems are an increasing reality in many environments, and both technological and social forces promise to accelerate this trend. VLSI and other simplifications are making desktop computers powerful engines and collections of these can have an aggregate compute power equivalent to a very large machine, but at far less cost. Therefore, in those cases where any single computation does not require the very high speed of the large machine, the small ones can be far more economical. It is also much easier in most organizations to justify low cost purchases; thus the result is often a rapid growth of investment in small computers, even without a rational evaluation of the economic advantage. The many advantages of desktop workstations, especially when coupled with larger mainframe machines for work which overflows the desk, are well known.

Unfortunately, it generally becomes necessary to make the resulting collection of computers work together smoothly, a daunting task not present in the single large machine case. This is the distributed computing problem. The LOCUS research effort, begun at UCLA in the late 1970s, attempted to understand how application software and computer networks should interact. The goal was to allow full network access to users who were "mere mortals", without special training. At the time, developing network software was so difficult that most people avoided it. The fundamental concept of *network transparency* grew out of these early efforts, and it was decided to try to build an actual transparent distributed operating system, both to demonstrate the feasibility of this concept, and also to provide a means to further understand its ramifications. By early 1981, a prototype system on a small collection of PDP-11s connected by an early ring network was operational. However, it wasn't until a year and a half later that enough of the associated technical problems and issues were understood and solved well enough that the system, then operational on VAXes, could be made generally available to users other than its original developers.

While many of the early users were enthusiastic in principle, they were far less happy with the non-product quality of the system. It was clear that the Locus approach had great utility but it was beyond the scope of a university research group to provide a finished production product.

Consequently, efforts were made to find a commercial vehicle to produce a product quality derivative of the concepts demonstrated by the research. Early in 1983, that work began at Locus Computing Corporation, an effort which would eventually encompass a number of different machine types, new concepts, largely reimplemented software, and a commitment of manpower and intensity which would dwarf that done earlier at UCLA.

There are several lessons worth learning from this experience. First, distributed functionality should be largely hidden from application programs and users. Providing a convenient distributed computing environment, as represented by a very high degree of transparency, is difficult. But, building software on top of such a base is essentially as easy as building for a single machine. Consequently, it is clear that these facilities ought to be provided in such a manner that maximum use of them may be made. An application should not be required to deal with knowing whether a resource it wishes to interact with is local or not, or knowing specialized means of interacting with remote resources, any more than high level language programmers should be required to write I/O channel programs, or overlays to provide the equivalent of virtual memory. The unnecessary cost and pain is inexcusable. The operating system is thus an appropriate vehicle for support of transparency.

Second, it is exceedingly difficult to reduce the elapsed time between the inception of a research idea and its commercial availability below the typical decade so often quoted. LOCUS has done better, but due only to a combination of vision within a major corporation, and an unusual level of dedication from its original conceivers and developers, many of whom participated in its entire history of maturation.

This book is intended to convey to the reader both the concepts which are key to the distributed system architecture, and "truth" in the form of an actual case study of what is required to support such functionality. The system as described in these pages has been fully operational for some time; ideas, however appealing on the surface, which were not successfully implemented in a product quality way, complete with error handling, integration with other features, and stability under a wide range of conditions are not included in the book.

In closing, it is difficult to convey how many things had to "go right", and how many people's enormously dedicated support was essential in order to develop these concepts and make a resulting system product publically available. The director and research managers at the U.S. Department of Defense research agency ARPA, staff at UCLA, and the dedicated Locus Computing Corporation team are obvious. Numerous people within IBM and especially the IBM Palo Alto Science Center have invested considerable effort in "making it happen". Heartfelt thanks to all.

Gerald J. Popek
Santa Monica, California
June 1985

Acknowledgments

The LOCUS development was greatly aided by numbers of people, whose contributions have made an enormous difference. First, there are several designers and developers not otherwise mentioned in this book. Charles Kline participated in the original conception of LOCUS on a plane flight from Silicon Valley, and has been a significant intellectual force throughout the system's history. Evelyn Walton has contributed in countless ways, first at UCLA and then at Locus Computing Corporation. A number of students participated in spirited design sessions and built early code as part of the ARPA research effort.

The development team at Locus Computing Corporation has spent enormous energy, intellect, and dedication in both the hard and the never ending smaller tasks. They truly created Locus.

UCLA Computer Science provided a tolerant environment in which the original research work could proceed. Hundreds of students and staff exercised early versions of the system; later, thousands of students provided the half million connect hours that gave a certain measure of reality.

The first large scale LOCUS system at UCLA did not come about without effort. Terry Gray in particular, together with Doris McClure and others, had responsibility for creating and then operating a local area network composed of twenty Vaxes, in the days when Ethernets were objects of curiosity, LOCUS installation was still an art form, and system stability was a goal.

Several major corporations had a substantive positive effect; Xerox Palo Alto Research Center provided a fertile environment for early conceptual development; Digital Equipment Corporation provided a major subsidy for a large Vax network at UCLA. IBM provided the enormous support required to turn a prototype concept into a working system; including functionality extensions, documentation, quality assurance, service tools, and not least, increasing the understanding of what is required to achieve very high product standards.

The LOCUS Distributed System Architecture

1 The LOCUS Architecture

This document describes the LOCUS software architecture. The document is composed of a brief overview and roadmap through the report, an introduction to necessary concepts, and detailed architectural description.

1.1 Architectural Overview and Document Roadmap

The LOCUS operating system is a distributed version of Unix™, with extensive additional features to aid in distributed operation and support for high reliability and availability behavior. Many of these facilities are of substantial value even when LOCUS is used on single, standalone computers. LOCUS provides a surprising amount of functionality in a reasonably small package.

The system makes a collection of computers, whether they are workstations or mainframes, as easy to use as a single computer, by providing so significant a set of supports for the underlying network that it is virtually entirely invisible to users and applications programs. This *network transparency* dramatically reduces the cost of developing and maintaining software, and considerably improves the user model of the system. It also permits a great deal of system configuration flexibility, including diskless workstations, full duplex I/O to large mainframes, transparently shared peripherals, incremental growth over a large range of configurations (from one workstation to a large network of workstations and mainframes) with virtually *no* effect on applications software required to take advantage of the altered configuration. This transparency is supported even in a heterogeneous network of various cpu types. For example, if a user or program running on one machine type in a LOCUS network attempts to execute a program for which the only available version runs on a different machine type, LOCUS will automatically cause that execution to occur on the appropriate machine, completely transparently to the caller.

The LOCUS design also provides support by which the LOCUS user and his applications software can transparently access resources (programs, stored data, peripheral devices, etc.) on other machines not running the LOCUS system, in a reasonably transparent way. Conventional gateway software is also supported.

™ Unix is a trademark of AT&T Bell Laboratories.

The following sections provide a brief overview of the significant LOCUS features.

1.2   Transparent, Distributed Operation

The power of network transparency and compatibility with an existing operating system environment can hardly be overestimated. It is commonplace to observe that distributed computing is very important, both in the near and longer term future. It is less well understood that unless a wide collection of distributed system application software becomes rapidly available, the growth of distributed computing will be severely retarded. The LOCUS philosophy of very extensive transparency, together with Unix compatibility, even in distributed mode, means that programs which run on a single-machine Unix system will operate, without change, with their resources distributed. That is, one can take a standard application program, set a few configuration parameters, and cause it to execute with parts of the program running on one machine, parts on other machines, and both the data and devices which it accesses distributed throughout the LOCUS network, all without change to the application. This ability means that there is immediately available a very large collection of distributed application software, the necessary prerequisite to commercially effective distributed computing. LOCUS also includes a host of facilities to control where data is located and which users and machines can access data, peripherals, cpus, and logical resources.

1.3   High Reliability

Reliability and availability are key to applications envisioned for LOCUS for two general reasons. First, many of the applications themselves demand a high level of reliability and availability. For example, the effect of a machine failure for an office system user is the equivalent of randomly locking that user out of his office at a random point for an unknown duration, an unacceptable situation. Database requirements for reliable operation are well known. Second, the distributed environment presents serious new sources of failures, and the mechanisms needed to cope with them are more difficult to construct than in single-machine environments. To require each application to solve these problems is a considerable burden. LOCUS provides advanced facilities for both the local and distributed environment which operate transparently. These facilities include a filesystem which guarantees that, even in the face of all manner of failures, each file will be retained in a consistent state, either completely updated, or unchanged, even if alterations were in progress at the time of failure. This *commit* mechanism generally involves no additional I/O and so performs very well.

One of the important reliability and availability features of LOCUS is its support for automatic replication of stored data, with the degree of replication dynamically under user control. Loss of a copy of a replicated file need not affect continued operation. Redundancy checks are included to avoid propagation of errors. These reliability and availability facilities are among the most advanced in the industry, and they are provided at exceedingly low cost. No special hardware is required; they may all be made available merely by putting LOCUS on the computers of interest.

1.4 High Performance

It would be most desirable if a distributed system has at least the following performance characteristics:

a. Access to resources when all resources are local performs approximately as well as would be the case if the mechanisms for remote access were not present. In the case of LOCUS, one desires that a program running under LOCUS, with all resources residing locally, performs as well as that same program running under Unix.

b. Remote access, while by necessity slower than local access, should be reasonably comparable to local access. If this (rather ambitious) goal can be achieved, then many issues regarding where resources should be located to optimize performance can be ignored. It should be noted that such a performance goal is far more aggressive than is typically achieved by conventional layered distributed systems.

LOCUS achieves both these goals, and is virtually unique in doing so. This level of networked performance compares exceedingly favorably with layered protocol implementations for remote access.

1.5 Unix Compatibility

LOCUS has been derived from Unix by successive modification of its internals by and considerable extension. For virtually all applications code, the LOCUS system can provide complete compatibility, at the object code level, with both Berkeley Unix and System V, and significant facilities are present to provide high degrees of compatibility with other versions of Unix as well. As a result, one routinely takes unrecompiled load modules from other Unix systems and runs them unchanged on LOCUS. The process of converting an existing Unix system to LOCUS is designed to be a largely automated step of removing the Unix kernel and associated software, inserting the LOCUS kernel with its supporting system software, and reformatting secondary storage to add the reliability facilities and functional enhancements.

1.6   Heterogeneous Machines and Systems

LOCUS contains a set of facilities that permits different cpu types to be connected in a single LOCUS system. A high degree of transparency is supported across the various machines. For example, attempts to execute programs prepared for different cpus will automatically cause execution on the appropriate target machine, all transparently to the calling program or user. Such sophisticated transparency is accomplished in a manner that does not add complexity to the user view of the system.

1.7   Guide to This Document

This document is intended for both the system designer who is familiar with principles of distributed processing, as well as those with more general background. Chapter 2 therefore contains a discussion of important distributed computing concepts, which is recommended to anyone not familiar with transparency, support for heterogeneity, and associated issues. Chapter 3 begins the presentation of the LOCUS architecture itself. It concentrates on the LOCUS distributed filesystem, and includes considerable detailed information regarding implementation. Chapter 4 describes how distributed process execution is done, including synchronization of access to shared resources. The filesystem and distributed tasking are basic to the LOCUS architecture and support of transparency.

Since a distributed facility can be dynamically affected by failures or planned addition or deletion of participating computers, LOCUS provides a general dynamic reconfiguration facility. It is described in Chapter 5. Chapter 6 describes the facilities present in LOCUS to permit transparent interconnection of heterogeneous computers. The important case supported is different cpu types within a LOCUS network. The mechanisms are fairly general and apply to a significant collection of system types. Chapter 7 lays out the system management tools provided along with the basic distributed operating system. There are two sets of tools. The first permits control of resources in a decentralized manner during normal operation, and the second aids in adding sites to a LOCUS network—either by introducing new ones, or converting previously existing conventional single-machine Unix systems.

Two appendices are included. The first lists the system calls that were added to the application view of Unix. Those functions provide the means by which programs may exert detailed control over distributed operation. The second appendix describes the LOCUS network messages. They are an example of a full distributed system protocol, and are presented in a manner independent of the underlying transmission medium.

The level of detail varies considerably throughout the document. That was done so that the architecture could be described at a fairly general level, while at the same time giving considerable concrete information to demonstrate feasibility when appropriate.

2 Distributed Operation and Transparency

It is well known that the cost of software development and maintenance is an increasing component of the cost of supporting computing systems today. Also, the connection of machines into various forms of distributed computing systems is an accelerating trend which is widely recognized to have just begun. What is not as widely appreciated however, is that this second trend significantly exacerbates the first; that is, distributed software is generally far more difficult to develop, debug, and maintain than single-machine software. There are several reasons. First the way in which a user or a program used to access remote resources, be they data, programs, or tasks, was different from (and more complex than) local resource access. For example, a local file is typically accessed through *open, close, read,* or *write* calls, while remote access required execution of a file transfer protocol, accompanied by renaming of that file.

Second, the error modes present in distributed systems are richer and often more frequent than those present in single-machine systems. For example, *partial failure* of a distributed computation can easily occur in a distributed environment, since one of the participating machines may fail while the others continue unaware. By contrast, in a single-machine environment, both programmers and users generally expect that a failure will stop their entire computation.

Third, in long-haul networks, the bandwidth of the network is typically limited and the delay is considerable, especially when compared to analogous parameters within a machine connected to the network. Local nets, by contrast, provide connections where the bandwidth and delay characteristics, while still considerably inferior to those within a mainframe, are dramatically better than the long-haul case. The local net may have capacity and performance which is 3-10% of the internal bus of machines that are interconnected by it. One expects that since local networking is immature, further improvement is quite possible.

This bandwidth/delay improvement of between one and two orders of magnitude, accompanied by substantial cost reductions, permits one to seriously rethink the means by which systems are interconnected at the various software levels. One of the most significant results of such an effort is the concept of making the network of no concern, i.e., invisible, to most users and applications.

In the next sections, we examine the concept of such *transparency* and motivate its desirability. Then methods of realizing transparency are discussed and compared. Limits to transparency are pointed out, and their impact evaluated. Finally, conclusions regarding the proper role of transparency in local area, long-haul, and low-speed networks are offered.

2.1 The Concept of Transparency

We have already pointed out the unpleasant truth of distributed systems: software in that environment, especially for true distributed applications, is often far harder to design, implement, debug, and maintain than the analogous software written for a centralized system. The reasons — the errors/failures problem and issues of heterogeneity — have also already been mentioned.

Many of these problems need not be intrinsic to the application view of distributed systems, however. It may be perfectly reasonable to open a file in precisely the same manner independent of whether the file is local or remote; i.e., issue the same system call, with the same parameters in the same order, etc. That is, the syntax and semantics of services should not be affected by whether or not a given function involves local or remote support. If *open (file-name)* is used to access local files, it also is used to access remote files. That is, the network becomes "invisible," analogous to the way that virtual memory hides secondary store. Hiding the existence of the network, at least so far as the nature of interfaces is concerned, can greatly ease software development.

This solution is called *network transparency;* all resources are accessed in the same manner independent of their location.

Of course, one still needs some way to control resource location for optimization purposes, but that control should be separated from the syntax and semantics of the system calls used to *access* the resources. That is, the existence of the network should not concern the user or application programs in the way that resources are accessed. Ideally then, one would like the graceful behavior of an integrated storage and processing system for the entire network while still retaining the many advantages of the distributed system architecture. If such a goal could be achieved, its advantages would include the following.

    a. *Easier software development.* Since there is only one way to access resources,

and the details of moving data across the network are built-in, individual software
packages do not require special-purpose software for this purpose. Functions are
location independent.[1]

b. *Incremental Change Supported.* Changes made below the level of the network-
   wide storage system are not visible to application software. Therefore, changes in
   resource support can be made more easily.

c. *Potential for Increased Reliability.* Local networks, with a fair level of
   redundancy of resources (both hardware and stored data), possess considerable
   potential for reliable, available operation. However, if this potential is to be
   realized, it must be possible to easily substitute various resources for one another
   (including processors, copies of files and programs, etc.). A uniform interface
   which hides the binding of those resources to programs would seem to be
   necessary if the higher reliability goal is to be realized.

d. *Simpler User Model.* By taking care of the details of managing the network, the
   user sees a conceptually simpler storage facility, composed merely of files,
   without machine boundaries, replicated copies, etc. The same is true for other
   resources visible to the user. Therefore, when moving from a simple machine to
   multisite operation, the user view is not needlessly disturbed.

In the next sections, we outline principles of network transparency and associated
design issues that arise. Subsequently, we point out that full transparency is not
achievable, or even desirable, in practice. Nevertheless, exceptions must be made with
great care, in order not to destroy the benefits transparency is designed (and able) to
provide.

---

[1] On the local network used to develop a LOCUS prototype, the first version of network software made the
network appear like another Arpanet, in which the details of the network are visible to application
programs. The construction of a network-wide printer daemon required over 20 processes and several
thousand lines of code beyond the spooler function itself to deal with error conditions, size problems, and
asynchronous events. Once the network-transparent LOCUS system was installed, virtually all of this
mechanism vanished.

2.2   Dimensions to Transparency

There are a number of aspects to network transparency. First is the manner in which objects and resources are named. Clearly, each object (such as a file) must have a globally unique name from the application point of view. In particular, the meaning of a name, i.e., the object with which it is associated, should not depend on the site in the network from which it is issued. This characteristic is called *name transparency*. Without it, moving or distributing software in the network can be very painful, since the effect of the program changes with the move.

Second, is the location of the resource encoded in the name? This is often the approach taken in early systems; the site name would be prepended to the existing filename to provide uniqueness. However, this choice has the unfortunate effect of making it quite difficult to move a file. The reason is that it is common to embed filenames in programs. Moving a file implies changing its name, making previously correct software no longer operational. The challenge, of course, is to provide *location transparency* in an efficient way, without significant system overhead to find the nodes storing the file. Some additional mechanism is necessary, since location would no longer be discernible from inspection of the name of the object.

In addition, automatically replicated storage is one important way that a system can increase effective reliability and availability to the user. To do so transparently, it is essential that the location of an object not be reflected in the name, since then it would be rather difficult to store a copy of the object at more than one site, and have any copy accessed automatically when others were not available.

Semantic consistency is a third important issue. By this we mean that system services, support libraries, commonly used application programs, and the like have the same effect independent of the site on which they are executed. This property is obviously essential if one is to be able to move program execution and data storage sites — a critical facility for the sake of reliability and availability methods. However, it is also very important from the viewpoint of managing software maintenance. If multiple versions of software are needed to compensate for subtle differences in environments, the maintenance problem grows significantly.

Actually, this environment consistency problem is an old one. People commonly complain that it is not possible to directly transport software even between two identical hardware environments, because of local changes to the operating systems, because of differences in location or naming of libraries and other application services, or even because of differences between the versions of software currently installed. While this compatibility issue is serious enough among unconnected installations, it is far worse in a distributed system, where a much more intimate mode of cooperation among sites is likely to be the rule.

Unfortunately, this issue of semantic consistency conflicts with goals of local autonomy, because it constrains the conditions under which individual sites install new software and customize existing facilities. Methods by which this conflict can be reconciled are outlined later.

2.3   Transparency and System Levels

There are many levels within a distributed system at which one could choose to provide transparency. One could build a true distributed operating system, for example, in which the existence of the network is largely hidden near the device driver level in the operating system nucleus. Alternatively, one could construct a layer of software over the operating systems but below application software. That layer would be responsible for dealing with distribution issues and functions. These first two approaches probably look very similar to users. Or, one could instead provide transparency via an extended programming language; those who wrote in that language would enjoy a network-wide virtual programming environment. Lastly, one might build transparency into an important application subsystem, such as a database. All of these methods have been or are being pursued. Below, we briefly comment on various of these approaches.

2.3.1   Transparency Via The Distributed Database

Most developers of distributed database systems mean by that label that the user of the distributed database system sees what appears to be a system-wide transparent database. Queries are expressed in the same manner as when all the data is resident on a single machine. The database system is responsible for keeping track of where the data is, and processing the query, including any optimization which may be appropriate. A distributed database can be built on top of multiple copies of identical single-machine operating systems, or it may even be constructed on top of a set of differing operating systems. The latter case may imply multiple implementations, of course. In some cases one may put an additional layer on top of existing heterogeneous database systems, to provide yet again another, albeit common, interface. Each of these approaches has been followed in practice.

2.3.2   Programming Language Supported Transparency

As an alternate approach to transparency, one could provide distribution mechanisms in a suitable programming language. Argus is an example of such an approach. In addition to providing primitives in the language to facilitate the construction of distributed programs that actually use the available parallelism, the language compiler and runtime system are responsible for providing many of the services that will be outlined in this chapter.

In particular, some developers have proposed some form of a *remote procedure call* as the central approach to transparency in distributed systems. In that view, a procedure call should have the same semantics (and syntax) whether the called procedure is to be executed locally or remotely. Sometimes restrictions on the remote case are imposed, such as forbidding the sharing of global variables among procedures that can be executed on differing sites. With this restriction, all data exchanged between the calling and called procedure are passed as explicit arguments. It has been shown that, with special protocols and microcode, even shared globals can often be supported in a local area network without serious performance degradation. Nevertheless, providing suitable semantics for remote procedure calls is a difficult task in the face of failures. Argus treats each call as a complete transaction.

2.3.3   The Operating System Level

In our judgment, however, if it is feasible within the constraints of existing systems, or if such constraints do not exist, it is more attractive to provide transparency at the operating system level rather than only via the alternatives mentioned above. In this way, all clients, including the database and language processor, can capitalize on the supporting facilities, customizing them as appropriate. Much of the work required to provide transparency is the same, independent of the level at which it is done. A global name map mechanism is needed. Intertask communication across the network must be supported in a standardized way. Distributed recovery is important. Given that there is substantial work to be done, it is highly desirable that the results of that work be available to as many clients as possible. Putting transparency only into the dbms or the language means that users not accessing the database, or programs not written in the extended language, do not have access to these desirable facilities. This situation is especially regrettable when *part* of a given function is built using the transparent facilities, but the rest cannot be, because it has been written in a different language, or must use other than the dbms or language functions.

For these reasons, in those few cases in this chapter where it is necessary to assume a context, we will couch our discussion in operating systems terms. The only significant case where this view is apparent is in the naming discussion, where we assume that the underlying name service structure is an extended *directory system,* rather than some other representation of the name-to-location mapping.

2.4 Optimization Control

One of the functions that conventional, nontransparent systems provide is the ability of applications to take explicit network-related actions for the sake of optimization. Placing a given file at a particular site, or moving a resource from one site to another, are obvious examples. In a distributed environment, one in general has the choice of moving the data to the process or the process to the data. When location of resources are explicitly part of the application interface, then it is generally clear how to take site-dependent actions. However, when a high level of transparency is provided, location of resources is by definition not apparent to the program. Unless some means are provided in a transparent environment to accomplish the same optimization actions, one could fairly expect significant performance difficulties, even in a local network.

The principle by which this optimization goal can be accomplished is straightforward. One can think of the set of functions by which the distributed system provides service to applications as an *effect language.* This language in the typical case is composed of a set of system calls; in some cases a more extensive JCL is also supplied as part of the system interface. We argue that a separate *optimization language* should be created, "orthogonal" to the effect language. The optimization language is *semantics free,* in the sense that whatever is stated in the optimization language cannot affect the outcome of a program; i.e., cannot change the result of any statement or series of statements in the effect language. The optimization language permits one to determine the location of resources, request that the system move a resource, etc. Since in a transparent system such actions do not affect the manner by which resources are accessed by applications, it is straightforward to make the optimization language free of semantic effect. In the case of a distributed operating system, this orthogonal language might consist of additional system calls such as:

>*my_loc* returns the site name at which the call is made;
>*object_loc (object_name);* returns the site name of the named object *make_near*
>*(object_name, site_name);* tries to move *object_name* to a site where access
>>from site *site_name* will be efficient.

With this kind of interface, a program such as the fragment below executes correctly whether or not the optimization commands are successfully performed by the system.

>*x = my_loc;*
>*make_near (file_foo, x);*
>*open (file_foo);*

The same advantages accrue to operations such as interprocess communication, system management, etc.

Note that the total set of system calls is available to a given program, so that it is certainly possible to create a program which will behave differently depending on the site of execution (i.e., not in a transparent manner). Consider the following program fragment:

>*if object_loc (file_foo) = my_loc*
>>*then call x else call y*

We consider the above a necessary dimension to the transparency concept.

This general view of orthogonal languages applies equally well to programming language based approaches to distributed systems. The effect language is the normal procedure language, as extended for example to provide tools for parallel execution. The optimization language represents an additional set of extensions that are nonprocedural, as declarations are, but which in this case do not affect the meaning of the program.

Another way of viewing this semantics-free optimization language is that if the
system were to ignore the commands, the program would still work correctly. In fact the
system might do just that if, for example, the application asked for a file to be made
local, but there were not enough room on the local storage medium. Lastly, as indicated
above, if the application really wishes not to run unless its optimization commands were
successful, it should be straightforward to do so.

2.5 Naming

As we saw earlier, naming is a key component of transparency. It is desirable that each
resource (data, processing agent, or device) be uniquely identified (name transparency)
so that uttering a given name always references the same resource. This form of
transparency allows software to migrate both before and during its execution. As we
shall see in this section, however, naming is a sophisticated issue, even in the single-site
situation, because name-to-resource translation is often context dependent.

Location transparency is a further dimension to transparency. To attain location
transparency one must avoid having resource location be part of the resource name. By
so doing, one is given the flexibility of transparently (*a*) moving resources from site to
site (akin to the flexibility data independence yields in transparently restructuring
database data); and (*b*) substituting one copy of a resource for another.

In this section we will investigate not only name and location transparency, but also
the area of contexts, some performance considerations, the role of resource replication
and certain local autonomy considerations.

2.5.1 Single Site Global Naming

Before considering naming in a multisite environment, consider the single site. One
would imagine that most single-site environments have unique resource naming
facilities. Nonetheless, the action of a given command may often be context dependent,
which is to say that the identical sequence of commands may not always have the same
effect. Such mechanisms are not new. The *working directory* facility in most tree-
structured filesystems is perhaps the best example. It provides a way of expanding
abbreviated pathnames to globally unique names. Each process, by setting its working
directory, changes the effect of names uttered by programs run in the process.

Another form of context is the use of aliasing. A user or process may have a translation table that is used in preprocessing names. Different users, then, can access different resources using the same name. The syntactic context in which a name is uttered can also be significant. Typing the word *who* in the context of a command may cause some extensive searching to find the load module. On the other hand, the word *who* in the context of the command *copy who to who.old* will not invoke the extensive searching, but may only look for something called *who* in the working directory.

So we see that even though global naming provides a means for uniquely identifying resources in a single-site system, there are several ways the context in which a name is uttered can influence which resource is accessed. Next we turn to the issue of contexts in a distributed environment.

2.5.2 Naming Contexts

Much of the mechanism needed to support transparency is concerned with name translation. Similarly, many of the ostensible problems with transparency also concern the way that a name is associated with an object. The distributed directory system alluded to in this chapter provides a system-wide decision about the association between object names and the objects themselves. A number of transparency problems can be avoided if it is possible to associate with a process or user a different set of decisions. We will call the preprocessing of names according to a set of per-user or process rules the application of a naming *context*.

Use of contexts can solve a set of problems in a network transparent distributed system. Consider the following issues:

a. Two network transparent systems that were developed independently using the same distributed operating system are subsequently merged. Clearly one must expect numbers of name conflicts; i.e., object *x* exists in both networks and refers to different files.

b. A set of programs is imported from another environment; different naming conventions were used there so changes are needed to run in the target distributed system. Source code may not be available. While this problems occurs today in single systems, one expects it to be more frequent in a large-scale transparent system with a single, fixed, naming hierarchy.

Both of these examples, as well as the temporary file problem mentioned below, have the characteristic that the global, hierarchical name structure provided by the distributed system did not meet the needs of individual programs.

Suppose by contrast it were possible to construct an efficient name map package on a per-program basis that is invoked whenever a name is issued. That package would convert the program-issued names to appropriate global system names. The database used by that package is the naming context within which the program is then run. There are many degrees of generality one might achieve with a context mechanism, from the simple working directory mentioned earlier, to IBM's JCL, to Unix shell aliases, to extensive *closure* mechanisms.

Here we are interested in aspects of such proposals which aid in solving distributed system problems like those mentioned above. What is needed is the ability to replace a partial string of components of a pathname with a different string of components. For example, in the case of merging two networks, a process might issue the name /bin/special.program, and the context mechanism might convert that name to /network1/bin/special.program, where /network1 is a network-wide directory which contains special programs needed for software developed in network1 that use library filenames incompatible with naming conventions in network2. Definition of contexts should be loadable and changeable under program control. Contexts can be stored in files in the global directory system. A default context can be invoked at user login time.

2.5.3 Local Data

There are numbers of situations where, for the sake of significantly improved performance, or to ease operational problems, it may be desirable to make a few exceptions to complete transparency. In Unix, for example, it is conventional for the /tmp directory to be used for temporary storage needed by running programs. Typically, any user may read or write into that directory, creating files as necessary. Programs have pathnames embedded into their code which generate and use files in /tmp. It is rare that any files in /tmp are shared among disparate users. The question arises: should /tmp be treated as just another globally known directory in the network-wide naming system? If so, there will be the unavoidable overheads of synchronizing access to files in that directory, maintaining consistency among multiple copies if they exist, etc. Is the /tmp *directory* itself highly replicated? If so, these overheads can be significant. If not, then when most sites create a temporary file, that creation will involve a remote directory update. These costs will be frequently incurred, and generally unnecessarily.

Alternately, one could introduce the concept of *local file directories*. A local file directory is not network transparent. A directory of that name exists on each node, and files created in that directory are accessible only from that node. /tmp/foo on site i and /tmp/foo on site j are different files. Since this local file directory is not replicated and not globally known, access can be faster and inexpensive. Sun's NFS effectively uses this solution. One could even give each local directory two names. One name is the common shared name: /tmp in the above example. Each such directory would also have a global, network transparent name as well — /tmpi and /tmpj for example — so that if necessary, temporary files could be remotely accessed in a transparent fashion.

Such a compromise induces problems, however, and should not be generally used. It makes process transparency very difficult to achieve, for example. Two programs which run successfully on the same site, exchanging data through temporary files, will not run if separated. There are many better solutions to the desire to avoid overhead in the support of temporary files that do not involve compromising transparency. For example, the context mechanism discussed below can be used to cause temporary filenames issued by a program to be mapped to a (globally available, network transparent) directory which happens to be locally or near-locally stored, and not replicated.

The desire for site-dependent naming is also raised by system initialization issues. Once the basic system is booted on a node, a program which finishes initialization work may wish to open a file which contains local configuration parameters. That initialization program wishes to be simple. If the initialization directory is a local directory, then the identical copy of the initialization program could be run on each site with the appropriate effect. This motivation is especially strong if an existing, single-site program is being adapted for use in the distributed environment. A better solution is to add to the system a call that permits a program to determine what site it is running on, for then the calling program can compose a specific (global, network transparent) filename from that information. Such a mechanism can be used to get the desired effect.

2.6   Heterogeneity

Despite the clear and overriding advantages to transparency, there are several intrinsic limitations in certain environments to making the network system entirely transparent. The problems are presented by heterogeneity of hardware and software interfaces. Additional problems that are often mentioned, such as local autonomy, dynamic optimization desires, or the necessity to support slow links connecting subnets themselves connected by local area technology, are of far less importance in our judgement. Each of these issues is discussed below.

2.6.1   Hardware Heterogeneity

Differences in hardware among the machines connected to the network fall into several major categories. First, the instruction sets of the machines may differ. This means that a load module for one machine cannot be executed on another, incompatible machine. A distributed system which required the user (or his program) to issue one name to get a function done when executing on one machine, but another name for the same function when execution is to occur on another machine, is not transparent. What one really wants in this case is for a single application-visible name to be mapped to multiple objects, with the choice of mapping and execution site (including shipping of needed data) to be automatically done in a way that depends on external conditions. However, this one-to-many mapping must be set up carefully, as there are other times when the individual objects need to be named individually (when a load module is to be replaced, for example).

Second, while differences in instruction sets can be hidden via methods inspired by the above considerations, incompatibilities in data representations are more difficult to handle. Suppose, for example, that program x, for which there exists a load module only for machine type X, wishes to operate on data produced by program y, which runs only on machine type Y. Unfortunately, the machines involved are VAXes and M68000s, and the data includes character arrays. The M68000, with 16-bit words, is byte-addressable, and if the high-order byte of a word has address i, then the low-order byte has address i+1. The VAX, also byte-addressable, addresses bytes within a word in the reverse order. Since both instruction sets enforce the corresponding conventions, attempts to index through the character array will have different effects on the two machines. As a result, it is not possible in general to provide transparent access to that data. Differences in floating point formats are another well-known example, which may be diminished by impending standards. Incompatibilities in higher level data structures are usually not an intrinsic problem, as those are generally induced by compiler conventions which can be altered to conform to a common representation. Nevertheless, reaching such an agreement can be rather difficult, and there is always the remaining problem of compatibility with the past. Strong data typing can help, but this facility is not currently in use outside of a few programming languages. In the Unix context, much data exchange *among* programs is via ascii text strings, which can be automatically supported in a transparent way, further alleviating the problem.

The third dimension of hardware incompatibility concerns configurations. While the cpus may be functionally identical, one system may have more space, either in main or secondary store, or may have certain attached peripherals essential to execution. This problem is generally relatively minor. The availability of virtual memory on most machines, even microprocessor chips, relieves the main store problem, and a good distributed filesystem can hide secondary store boundaries. The other problems can largely be treated in a way similar to the incompatible instruction set issue, that is, by automatically and invisibly causing the invoked program to be run on a suitable configuration if one exists in the network.

Hence, we conclude that hardware heterogeneity, with the exception of data representation problems, presents no significant obstacle to complete transparency.

2.6.2 Operating System Heterogeneity

While hardware issues can largely be handled by suitable techniques, if there are requirements to support more than one operating system interface in the transparent distributed system, serious problems can arise. The issue is *not* the heterogeneity of the system call interface of and by itself. After all, many systems today support more than one such interface. Usually, one set of system calls is considered native, and the others are supported by an emulation package which translates the additional set of system calls into the corresponding native ones. That approach is usually taken because it is architecturally simple and because most of the expected load will use the native set. There is no particular need to favor one set over the other so far as the internal implementation is concerned, however. In fact, one could even support one system call interface on one machine, another on a different set of machines, and automatically cause a given load module to be executed on the appropriate machine, much in the same manner as done to support heterogeneous cpu instruction sets. (After all, system calls are merely extensions to the basic set of instructions anyway.)

2.6.3 File System Heterogeneity

Many of the significant problems in operating systems heterogeneity occur in the filesystems, for it is there that each system provides an environment which must be globally visible. Thus the nature of the parameters with which one requests functions from the filesystem is paramount. Unless the filesystem models are closely compatible, trouble results. Consider an item so simple as the nature of a filename. In Unix, a filename is hierarchical, with each element of the path composed from virtually any ascii character except '/', which is used to separate elements of the pathname. While the DEC-VAX VMS filesystem superficially presents a hierarchical pathname to applications as well, the first component is a device name (followed by a ':') and the last component is of the form xxxxxx.xxx. Any component is of limited length. As a result, while Unix programs can generate and use any VMS filename, the reverse is not true. If one tries to glue one tree into the other as a subtree, many attempts to create or use files will fail. If the two hierarchies are combined with a new "super root," then those problems still remain, and in addition, any program which used to give what it thought was a complete pathname is now missing the initial component (although this is just one more historical problem). Alternatively, one can build a general-purpose map mechanism that takes a symbolic pathname in one naming system and maps it to a name in the other. This approach can give a high level of transparency, but it suffers from the performance degradation implied by the necessity to use bidirectional maps and keep them consistent. This cost need not be great in terms of overall system performance if filesystem *opens* are relatively rare. However, this map is one of the architectural structures which contributed to the National Software Works project's poor performance. Still other approaches, based on careful use of contexts, are possible when the target operating systems can be altered to provide richer mechanisms.

One also encounters significant differences in the semantics of filesystem operations and the file types supported. Even if both systems support such types as sequential, multi-indexed, etc., it is often the case that the details of the types differ. For example, one indexed file type might permit variable length keys but no duplicates, while the other supports the reverse. This problem is not really as serious as it may seem at first glance.

In fact, it is not strictly a transparency issue since it occurs in single-machine systems, in the sense that a single-site operating system may support a set of file types that are not mutually compatible. In the distributed case we are considering, we merely have a larger set of file types. Of course, it is unpleasant in any environment to have two nearly the same but incompatible facilities.

File system semantic incompatibility is further increased by emerging desires to see such functions as transaction support and multi-object commit supported in the basic system for use across multiple programs, rather than being limited to the database, for example.

Interprocess communication is one more important issue. The conventions by which processes dynamically exchange information in a system is another area where lack of agreement causes trouble. If the operating systems across which transparency is desired use ipc mechanisms that cannot be reasonably mapped one to the other, then the situation is not unlike that of multiple similar access types in the filesystem.

2.7 Error Modes

It is the conventional wisdom that distributed systems present a significantly richer set of errors to the application and user, and for this reason complete transparency is not possible. In general, that statement is of course true. Individual nodes can fail, taking parts of computations with them which cannot be repeated elsewhere because of special, now lost, resources. However, in our experience, the error situation in distributed systems is often not nearly so complex, for two principal reasons. First, many of the failures in a distributed environment map well into failure modes which already existed in single machine systems. It might be useful to add additional error codes so that the program involved has additional information, but that is hardly a serious change. Even with the additional information, the program's options may be quite limited. For example, if two programs are cooperating, exchanging data, and altering their own states (i.e., their local memory) as a result of data received from the other program, then if one of the pair is destroyed due its host system failing, the other program in most cases will just have to abort.

Second, the additional mechanisms being added to distributed systems to address the admittedly richer error environment are also appropriate for, and are being added to, single-machine systems. A good example is the transaction concept. Transactions provide a uniform set of tools for controlling the effect of failures in the distributed environment. Nested transactions have been proposed to limit the effect of failure within a transaction, and a prototype implementation exists for LOCUS. Flat transactions have been implemented on single-machine systems for some time.

Nevertheless, there are significant differences between errors in the distributed environment and a centralized system, and they can show up in somewhat subtle ways. For example, some errors which are often received immediately in a single-machine environment might be received asynchronously, delayed by some amount, in the distributed system. Suppose there is no space on a disk for pages being written by a user process. In a single-machine system, an attempt to write the first overflow page generally will cause the application to be immediately signaled. However, in a distributed system, it is rather difficult for the system to notify the user immediately, as there are various delays and buffering in the path from user to remote disk, and from remote machine back to the user. It is quite easy for the user to have written a substantial number of pages before receiving word that none of them can be stored.[1] It is unreasonable to expect that the system will give explicit acknowledgement after each write, as the round-trip time implied has unpleasant performance implications.

In this example, while the error is the same, the conditions under which it is reported differ, making the user-specific recovery options more difficult, since a substantial amount of data may have been lost. In the single machine system the user may have been able to keep a few buffers of data, so that in case of error that data could be written elsewhere. This case is an example of the "partial failure" problem mentioned earlier, but here one of the processes involved was the system, while the application continued unaware.

---

[1] This is especially the case if the system maintains global buffer pools at each site and sends buffers across the net, or initiates writes to disk, only after the pools are filled. While this problem can occur in a single-machine system, the delay is worsened in the distributed environment.

Service outages also make it difficult to maintain completely the illusion of transparency. If communication between sites is lost, then it becomes painfully clear what resources are local and which are remote. There is no perfect solution to this problem; replication of resources helps, but if a replicated storage object is updated on both sides of a broken link, problems may result upon reconnection. If replication is incomplete, then loss of resources will still occur. The handling of partitioned operation when replicated resources are present is a substantial topic in its own right. Lastly, programs written for a single-machine environment may not be able to usefully deal with the error reports in the network, nor be able to use the added functions like transactions.

2.8   Local Autonomy and Transparency

It has been well recognized that while a distributed system interconnects a number of sites, those sites may wish to retain a considerable degree of control over the manner in which they operate. The desire for local autonomy is real, whether each site is a personal workstation or a large, multiuser system supporting an entire department of users.

One immediately wonders about the relationship between autonomy and transparency. There are multiple issues to be examined:

a. Resource control
b. Naming
c. Semantic consistency
d. Protection
e. Administration

The subject is substantial; here we only briefly touch on the major issues.

2.8.1   Resource Control

In many cases the machines interconnected in a distributed system are operated by different people (in the case of a network of personal computers) or by different parts of an organization (in the case of larger machines). Each of these different groups typically wishes to retain some significant level of control over resource use on its own systems. For example, the personal computer user may well be quite disconcerted if, in the middle of a cpu-intensive bitmap update to his screen, some other user in the network dispatched a large task to run on the first user's machine! Transparency makes such an action trivial to take.

The problem is not that transparency is bad; after all, such an action would be possible even through an awkward interface to foreign resources. Rather, resource control tools are needed in any distributed system that connects different administrative domains. Resource controls are also attractive as a way to handle system tuning and load control. If the nature of the controls that are desired is simple, then it may be possible to slightly extend the protection system to accomplish the desired goal. For example, storage space on the local disk could be limited by setting protection controls on the directories whose files are stored on that disk. Control over whether a given user can consume processing resources does require some extension, but in any case, these resource controls are not significantly different in principle from those typically found on multiuser single machine systems.

2.8.2 Naming

The naming problem occurs in the following way. Different users of even the same type of system may configure their directory systems in different ways; on one system the Fortran library is found under one name, while on another system it is elsewhere. If software from these two different systems are to be run in the context of a single, integrated name space, a conflict arises. To solve this problem, one must either force consistent name spaces or use contexts, as described earlier.

2.8.3 Semantic Consistency

This issue, mentioned early in this chapter, is one of the ways that transparency conflicts directly with local autonomy, as we already noted. However, contexts once again help, since the user who wishes to specify a different mapping of name to specific object can do so.

2.8.4 Protection

The protection problem has several dimensions in a distributed environment. First is the question of what protection controls are actually desired. Are access control lists needed, or will the <owner, group, public> mechanism found in many systems today suffice? We do not discuss this issue here, as it does not seriously impact the distributed system architecture. A second question, however, might. What should a given system trust? That is, machine x receives a message from machine y asking to have file *foo* opened on behalf of user *bar* and a set of pages replaced by updated ones. Should that message be believed? How much does machine x trust machine y? It has been argued that, at least at the database level, the most that should be believed is that the message came from machine y. X cannot be sure that the user is really *bar* because the remote software is not trustworthy. Here, we argue that all systems are running the same basic software, and so long as x is sure that machine y is running the standard system, the user authentication can be accepted, and there is no serious problem. Simple, encryption-based methods can easily be used to assure that x can tell that the software actually loaded at y is the standard approved version.[1] Note that the problem of protection in a distributed system is little different from a centralized system of commensurate size. This characteristic results from the fact that virtually all systems today, once they are connected by any reasonable functionality, permit remote access to exercise many of the protection failures on the local system that could have been exercised if the user had indeed been local. Thus the issue should be viewed as one concerning large, cooperating communities, rather than being peculiar to distributed implementations.

2.8.5 Administration

Large systems require administration and coordination. A distributed, transparent network is no exception. Statistics must be constantly gathered to monitor system operation, detect bottlenecks and failures, etc. Hardware and software must be maintained in a coordinated way. Mechanisms to accomplish these goals are needed, and must be installed and run in each of the participating systems, whether they are wanted or not.

2.9 Integration of Separate Networks

Despite the attractions of transparency, it is well recognized that when a given system must interface to the outside world (a distributed Unix net connected via SNA to IBM mainframes, say), it will not be feasible to maintain transparency. Hence the more traditional approach of explicit user and application visible protocols will remain. Given that is the case, one could argue that those protocols might as well be used in the local net too. This reduces development, since the transparent mechanism will not be needed. Further, since certain programs will have to operate in a distributed manner over the heterogeneous link, having transparency on one side of that link is no savings. Those

---

[1] Encrypt the system load module and a communication key. Decrypt that load module as part of the booting procedure. Employ the communication key for a digital signature on messages the node transmits. There are a few additional safeguards actually required to make this procedure safe.

programs might as well employ the single global network interface throughout.

This argument is naive. Much of the transparency mechanism is going to be built anyway by applications; to the extent possible it should be made universally available. In addition, there will certainly be many applications which will not be required to use the heterogeneous link. To force them to do so would be unfortunate indeed. Further, the hypothetical network application mentioned earlier already must use the single-machine interface anyway. The transparent extension can largely present the same.

A more interesting case occurs when one has several local networks, each transparent within itself, but where those networks are themselves interconnected by slow links on which a standard protocol such as X.25 or a lower level of SNA is run. How should resources on the distant network look to an application on the local net? We turn to this issue below.

2.9.1   Long-Haul and Low-Speed Networks

Geographically dispersed networks predominate in today's distributed computing environments. These systems do not provide a high degree of transparency, for three significant reasons. First, many of these networks connect a heterogeneous set of often vendor-supplied systems. It is frequently not practical to modify vendor-supported software, and even if it were, differences among the systems make the design of a transparent standard rather difficult. The National Software Works, mentioned earlier, is one such attempt, that layered a standard interface on top of the system, but below the application. Its incompleteness and poor performance have been noted.

A second important reason for the lack of transparency in existing networks concerns the manner in which they were developed. These systems are generally directly derived from early network architectures in which the most important task was to develop methods by which machines could communicate at all, rather than to take into account then poorly understood lessons of distributed computing. Third, long-haul networks typically represent a scarce resource. They are characterized by either low bandwidth or high delay, and usually by both. Therefore, it is quite appropriate in the view of many people to make that resource application visible through a different interface than the one through which local resources are seen.

The first issue, heterogeneity, undoubtedly will always be present; a high level of transparency in that case is not always feasible. However, when most of the computers of interest involve the same operating system interface, often the case in local networks or within a given organization, the heterogeneity issue is far less prevalent. The historical reason for the nature of cross system interfaces, while interesting, should not constrain new system architectures. Therefore, we are often left with the nature of the underlying transmission medium as the significant issue to be considered when evaluating the possibility of providing a high level of transparency in long-haul environments.

There is no doubt that the media are different; the long-haul environment presents far higher delay, much lower bandwidth, and significantly greater error rates than the local net. These differences make absolutely necessary a significant low-level protocol which is responsible for error handling (using acknowledgements, retransmission, sequence numbers, etc.), flow control, resource management, connection establishment, name mapping, data conversion, out-of-band signaling, and the like. These facilities are typically implemented in a multilayered protocol, meeting one of the several international or domestic standards.

Further, existing implementations provide an explicit interface to the network, permitting substantial control over its use. This characteristic is highly desirable, as the net is often a scarce resource, to be managed rather carefully.

However, it is our view that these issues do not conflict with the goal of transparency at all. First, just because a substantial set of protocol modules is needed to manage a complex device (the network) is not a reason to make the interface to the resources accessed through that device different from, and more awkward than, local resources. Similarly, one gives a simple open/close, read/write interface to local disks in conventional systems, rather than requiring one to write the complex channel program which ultimately does this work.

The desire for explicit resource control is real, however. Some mechanism is needed to accomplish that goal. We argue that the optimization language described earlier provides a suitable framework, at least from the individual user's point of view. Extensions to that language, to permit a system administrator to set more global resource management policies, undoubtedly will be needed in some environments.

The effect of this transparent approach to long-haul networks yields a picture composed of a number of local machine clusters, each cluster internally connected by a local area network, with the clusters interconnected by long-haul media. However, this view generates a number of internal architecture problems which must be solved. They include:

a. The unsuitability of such local net based algorithms as page faulting across the local network, as LOCUS does;

b. The flow control problems present in networks where fast and slow links are connected in series (long queues in front of the slow link back up into the fast links, blocking their use as well as associated resources such as buffers);

c. The need for considerable control over location of resources, for optimization reasons, beyond the often simple ones that can be tolerated in a local area environment.

However, these issues are relatively minor compared to the improvement which results from transparency.

2.10 Summary

This chapter has given a discussion of basic distributed system software concepts, independent of LOCUS. The remainder of this document concerns the LOCUS system itself.

3   The LOCUS Distributed Filesystem

The heart of the LOCUS architecture is its distributed filesystem. In this chapter, that architecture is described. The essential elements of the filesystem are its distributed naming catalog, the accompanying synchronization facilities, integrated replicated storage support, and the mechanisms to allow partitioned operation. First we present our general approach to remote access and remote service. Then we give a brief overview of the distributed filesystem, followed by a deeper discussion of the system data structures and the procedures used for normal operation. Methods used in LOCUS to synchronize simultaneous, distributed file access and modification are described. A section is devoted to filesystem support for interprocess communication, outlining the network-wide pipe mechanism. Next, the mechanisms involved in file replication are explained. Then we discuss the different ways in which the LOCUS architecture is structured for good performance. Finally, we end the chapter with some other filesystem-related functions.

3.1   Filesystem Overview

The LOCUS filesystem presents a single tree-structured naming hierarchy to users and applications. It is functionally a superset of the Unix tree-structured naming system. There are three major areas of extension. First, the single tree structure in LOCUS covers all objects in the filesystem on all machines. LOCUS names are fully transparent; it is not possible from the name of a resource to discern its location in the network. The critical importance of such properties was discussed in Chapter 2. The second direction of extension concerns replication. Files in LOCUS can be replicated to varying degrees, and it is the LOCUS system's responsibility to keep all copies up to date, and assure that access requests are served by the most recent available version. Third, LOCUS provides both the standard Unix, unsynchronized, file access policy as well as advisory and enforced locking. File and record locking is included in the architecture.

A substantial amount of the LOCUS filesystem design, as well as implementation, has been devoted to appropriate forms of error and failure management. These issues will be discussed throughout this chapter. Further, high performance has always been a critical goal. *In our view, solutions to all the other problems being addressed are really not solutions at all unless their performance is suitable.* In LOCUS, when resources are local, access is no more expensive than on a conventional Unix system. When resources are remote, access cost is higher, but dramatically better than traditional layered file transfer and remote terminal protocols permit.

The following sections discuss the internal system control flow, and then the static representation of a distributed LOCUS filesystem. Later sections show how that structure is used to provide transparent resource access.

3.2   Remote Service Control Flow

One of the goals of this product is to provide a high degree of transparency. Services which supplied access to or acted on local objects in the single machine case should be available for remote objects, and the service interface should be identical. Thus, if opening and reading local files were services provided via a procedure call interface into the operating system, the same calls should provide service on remote files. A strictly message-based service interface to remote service is clearly not consistent. Similarly, different procedure calls for remote vs. local service would be inappropriate. The model, then, must be of the form shown in Figure 3-1.

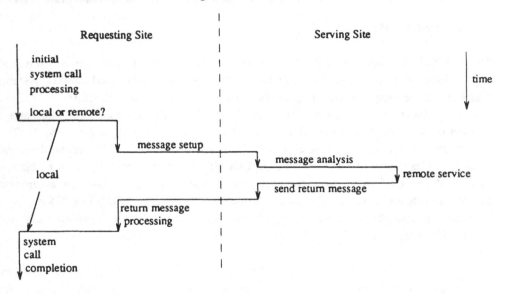

Figure 3-1: Processing a System Call

There are two components to network activity that should be considered independently. First, there is the network control — the formatting, queueing, transmitting and retransmitting. The traditional approach to network control is for a process to own the network device with requests for network activity being sent to that process, often causing some amount of data copying. Who would be making network requests? If it is an application program, then the network is clearly not transparent at that level. The only alternative is that the requests come directly from the operating system (prompted of course by some higher level action). To avoid the overhead of an application formatting a request and invoking the network control process, only to have it actually request the operating system to send some data, network control is incorporated by LOCUS into the operating system.

The second component of network activity is the service of foreign requests. Given that service requests are made below the operating system level, it is simpler for the service code to be entirely below that level as well, thereby prompting network service to be done within the operating system. Our model, then, is to communicate from operating system to operating system.

Within the framework of the environment already described, three approaches to support remote service are possible. First, one could pass the request up to an application-level process, as has been done historically. This approach is completely inappropriate in the proposed environment. The granularity of service is smaller than a system call and should consist entirely of kernel code. The overhead of passing a request to an application process, scheduling that process to be run, having it make the appropriate kernel call to do the work, passing the results back to this process, and having it send a response to the requesting operating system would dwarf the actual service code.

A second approach to the remote service problem takes the other extreme, which is to service the request entirely as part of the interrupt processing associated with the receipt of the request. This approach was seriously considered and would result in very good service time. However, it had two drawbacks. First, interrupts are asynchronous events that can suspend a process which was executing user-level or operating system code. Special care must be taken for each operating system data structure that the interrupt processor is now allowed to access while it is servicing a request. The system must guarantee that the interrupt processor sees a consistent state of these data structures; and thus any operating system code which manipulates these data structures must now be a critical section of code, run at an elevated processor priority which disables this interrupt from being processed. Certain data structures, such as disk buffers, already require manipulations to appear in critical sections since they are accessed by local, disk interrupt processors. This approach would increase the number of data structures which require special handling. Second, the service of a remote request required, in general, one or more input/output operations, which compared to processing speed could take a long time. One could not afford to have the processor waiting for such an event without doing other work. Consequently, the service would have to be suspended and continued after the I/O completed. Integrating such a facility into interrupt processing appeared to be complex. State information would have to be saved when a service request needed to do an I/O. Then many device interrupt routines would have to be changed so that when they noted an I/O completing as part of a remote service request, they could continue servicing the request. We rejected this approach due to the complexity of these two problems.

The solution chosen was to build a fast but limited process facility called *server processes*. These are processes which have no nonprivileged address space at all. All their code and stack are resident in the operating system nucleus. Any of their globals are part of the operating system nucleus's permanent storage. Server processes also can call internal system subroutines directly. As a result of this organization, the body of server processes is quite small; many types of messages are serviced with less than 30 lines of C code (some of which is comprised of subroutine calls to already existing system functions). As network requests arrive, they are placed in a system queue, and when a server process finishes an operation, it looks in the queue for more work to do. Each server process serially serves a request. The system is configured with some number of these processes at system initialization time, but that number is automatically and dynamically altered during system operation.

These lightweight processes permit efficient serving of network requests (therefore keeping protocol support cost low) while at the same time avoiding implementation of another structuring facility besides processes. In retrospect, this was an excellent early design decision, both because of the structuring simplicity which resulted, and because of the contribution to performance.

3.3 Static Picture of the Filesystem

In order to understand the LOCUS filesystem, it is helpful to examine the data structures that represent a functioning system. Below, we do so, first discussing the permanently stored structures, and then the dynamically maintained information in volatile memory.

The user and application program view of object names in LOCUS is analogous to a single, centralized Unix environment; virtually all objects appear with globally unique names in a single, uniform, hierarchical name space. Each object is known by its pathname in a tree,[1] with each element of the path being a character string. *There is only one logical root for the tree in the entire network.* Figure 3-2 gives a very small sample of a pathname tree. Note that the bold lines name the file /user/walker/mailbox.

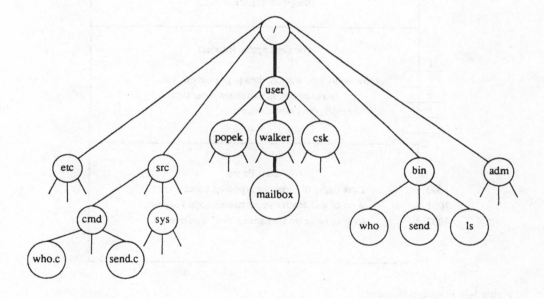

Figure 3-2: Hierarchical Naming

To a first approximation, the pathname tree is made up of a collection of *filegroups*, as in

---

[1] There are a few exceptions to the tree structure, provided by Unix-style links.

a conventional Unix environment.[1] Each group is a wholly self-contained subtree of the naming hierarchy, including storage for all files and directories contained in the subtree. Connections among subtrees compose a "supertree," where the nodes are filegroups.

A filegroup is implemented as a section of mass storage, composed primarily of a small set of file descriptors (called inodes) which serve as a low-level internal "directory," and a large number of standard size data blocks. A file is composed of an inode and an associated ordered collection of data blocks. These are used both for leaf or regular file data, and intermediate node or directory file data. One of the directories is treated as the root of the subtree for this filegroup. Figure 3-3 sketches the contents of a filegroup.

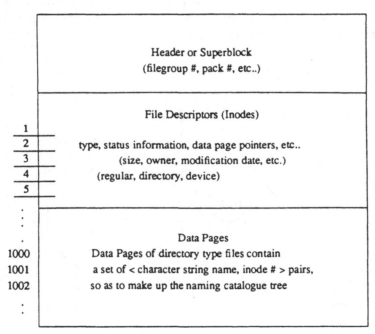

Figure 3-3: Filegroup Structure

Gluing together a collection of filegroups to construct the uniform naming tree is done via the *mount* mechanism. So far, this portrait is no different from normal Unix. However, the structure of filegroups and their interrelationships is actually more

---

[1] The term *filegroup* in this chapter corresponds directly to the Unix term *filesystem*.

sophisticated in LOCUS than Unix. That is partly due to the presence of mechanisms for remote operation, but a significant amount of the additional mechanism and data structuring is also present to support replication. We therefore turn to the subject of replication now.

3.3.1   Replication

Replication of storage in a distributed filesystem serves multiple purposes. First, from the users' point of view, multiple copies of data resources provide the opportunity for substantially increased availability.

From the system point of view, some form of replication is more than convenient; it is absolutely essential for system data structures, both for availability and performance. Consider a file directory. A hierarchical name space in a distributed environment implies that some directories will have filename entries in them that refer to files on differing machines. There are powerful motivations for storing a copy of all the directory entries in the path from the naming root to a given file local to the site where the file itself is stored, or at least "nearby." Availability is one clear reason. If a directory in the naming path to a file is not accessible because of network partition or site failure, then that file *cannot be accessed,* even though it may be stored locally. Second, directories in general experience a high level of shared read access compared to update. This characteristic is precisely the one for which a high degree of replicated storage will improve system performance.

Support for replicated storage presents a host of issues. One needs highly efficient but themselves replicated mapping tables to find copies of the replicated objects, and those mapping tables must be kept consistent and up-to-date. Suitable action in the face of failures, to maintain consistent copies of the replicated object as well as the catalog mapping tables, is necessary. It is rather difficult to develop a simple solution to these problems while at the same time addressing the further problems imposed by goals of high availability and performance.

LOCUS replication is designed to:

a. Permit multiple copies at *different* sites, rather than being restricted to different media on the same machine, as in shadow disks.

b. Allow a flexible degree of replication and a reasonable freedom to designate where the copies should reside. A given file can be stored on just a single site, at several sites or at many sites, with the possibility of increasing or decreasing the number of copies after initial creation. The system is responsible for keeping all copies consistent and ensuring that access requests are satisfied by the most recent version.

c. Allow the user and application program to be as unaware as they wish of the replication system. In other words one can either let system defaults control the degree of replication and file location or one can interact and strategically place file copies.

d. Support high performance and smooth operation in the face of failures. For example, a running application with a given file open should not be disturbed when another copy of that file reappears in the network.

With these goals in mind, let us consider the static structure that allows replication.

File replication is made possible in LOCUS by having multiple physical containers for a logical filegroup. Any given logical filegroup may have a number of corresponding physical containers residing at various sites around the network. A given file belonging to logical filegroup X may be stored at any subset of the sites where there exists a physical container corresponding to X. Thus the entire logical filegroup is not replicated by each physical container as in a "hot shadow" type environment. Instead, to permit substantially increased flexibility, any physical container is incomplete;[1] it stores only a subset of the files in the subtree to which it corresponds. The situation is outlined in Figure 3-4.

From the implementation point of view, pieces of mass storage on different sites are named and maintained as containers for a given filegroup. Each container is assigned a unique *pack number,* and this number, along with the associated logical filegroup number, is kept in the physical container header (Unix superblock).

To simplify access and provide a basis for low-level communication about files, the various copies of a file are assigned the same file descriptor or inode number within the logical filegroup. Thus a file's globally unique low-level name is:

<logical filegroup number, file descriptor (inode) number>

and it is this name which most of the operating system uses. Figure 3-4 gives an introductory sketch of replicated filegroups and replicated files.

In the example, there are two physical containers corresponding to the logical filegroup. Note that:

a. The filegroup number is the same in both copies.

b. The pack numbers are different.

---

[1] The exception to this rule is the Primary Copy, which must be complete.

```
┌──────────────────────────────┐                    ┌──────────────────────────────┐
│   filegroup # 43             │                    │   filegroup # 43             │
│   pack # 1 (primary copy)    │   superblocks      │   pack # 2                   │
│   filegroup size = 80,000    │                    │   filegroup size = 40,000    │
│   inode size = 1000          │                    │   inode size = 1000          │
│ 2 status info and pg ptrs    │   inode          2 │ status info and pg ptrs      │
│ 3 status info and pg ptrs    │   blocks         3 │ null                         │
│ 4 null                       │                  4 │ null                         │
│          .                   │                    │          .                   │
│          .                   │   data             │          .                   │
│   79,000 data blocks         │   blocks           │   39,000 data blocks         │
└──────────────────────────────┘                    └──────────────────────────────┘
```

Note:
      - inode #2 is replicated with the same status information on both packs
      - inode #3 is not replicated

Figure 3-4: Two Packs For A Given Filegroup

c. Files replicated on the two packs have the same file status information in the corresponding inode slot.

d. Any file can be stored either on the primary pack or on both.

e. Page pointers are not global, but instead maintained local to each pack. References over the network always use logical page numbers and not physical block numbers.

f. The number of inodes on each physical container of the filegroup is the same so that any file can be replicated on any physical container of the filegroup;[1]

g. If a copy of a file is not stored on a given pack, the status information in that inode slot will so indicate.

h. The inode information stored with each copy contains enough history to determine which versions of a file dominate other versions.

---

[1] In the event that one wishes to have a small physical container of a large filegroup (i.e., store just a few of the files), one may not want to pay the overhead of being able to store all the inodes. In that case it is straightforward to build an indirection mechanism that maps global inode numbers to the smaller local space.

The advantages of this replication architecture include:

    a.   Globally unique low-level names are implemented, so that high-to-low-level name translation need happen only once in a file access. Intermachine network traffic uses this efficient name.

    b.   Physical containers can be different sizes.

    c.   A given file need not be replicated, or may have as many physical copies as there are containers for the filegroup. The decision can be made on a per-file basis and the decision can change over time.

This design imposes the restriction that a copy of a file can reside only at those sites which host a pack for the filegroup.

Like Unix, LOCUS treats directories as a special type of file. A general replication mechanism was built for files, which normally operates in the same manner, independent of the file type.

In this section we have concentrated on the LOCUS structure within a single logical filegroup. We now move on to a discussion of how the supertree is created and maintained.

3.3.2   The Filegroup Mount Table

Logically mounting a filegroup attaches one tree (the filegroup being mounted) as a subtree within an already mounted tree. Figure 3-5a shows a filegroup with an empty directory *user*; Figure 3-5b shows the result of mounting a physical container for filegroup number 10 on top of /user. It is not a constraint that /user be an empty directory, but if it were not, the subtree subordinate to /user would become hidden and inaccessible after the mount operation.

The mount operation does not change any secondary storage information in either the mounted filegroup or the "mounted upon" filegroup. Instead, the glue which allows smooth path traversals up and down the expanded naming tree is kept as operating system state information. In standard, single-site Unix, a table is kept indicating where each filegroup is mounted. Further, the inode for the directory which is mounted over is kept in core at all times and marked so that requests concerning that directory will be indirected to the initial or root directory of the mounted filegroup.

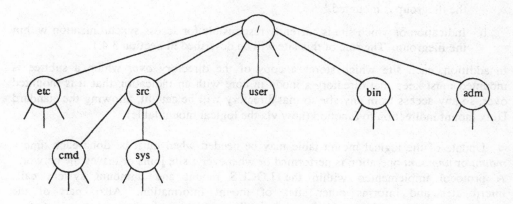

Figure 3-5a: Pathname Tree Before Mounting Filegroup 10

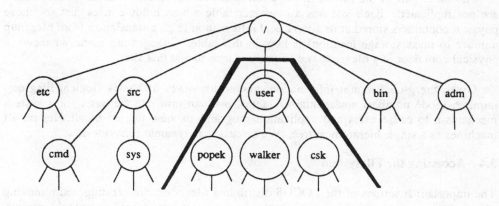

Figure 3-5b: Pathname Tree After Mounting Filegroup 10

In LOCUS this basic mechanism is expanded in several ways. Each machine must have a consistent and complete view of where filegroups are mounted: where in the naming hierarchy the subtree was placed, and which sites host containers for the filegroups. To maintain the expanded information, the mount table information was split into two tables. The *logical mount table* is globally replicated and contains, for each logical filegroup, the following information:

a. The logical filegroup number and the inode number of the directory over which the filegroup is mounted.[1]

b. Indication of which site is currently responsible for access synchronization within
the filegroup. The role of this site will be described in Section 3.4.1.

In addition, each site which stores a copy of the directory over which a subtree is
mounted must keep that directory's inode in core with an indication that it is mounted
over, so any access from any site to that directory will be caught, allowing the standard
Unix mount indirection to function (now via the logical mount table).

Update of the logical mount table may be needed when must be done each time a
mount or *unmount* operation is performed or whenever a site joins or leaves the network.
A protocol implemented within the LOCUS mount and unmount system calls
interrogates and informs other sites of mount information. Also, part of the
reconfiguration protocol reestablishes and distributes the logical mount table to all sites.

The other part of the mount information is stored in *container tables*. These tables
are not replicated. Each site has a container table which holds entries just for those
physical containers stored at its site. Local information (e.g., a translation from filegroup
number to mass storage location) is kept in this table. Changes are made whenever a
physical container of a filegroup (i.e., a pack) is mounted at that site.

Given the global mount information, unique low-level filenames (logical filegroup
number, inode number), and container tables, one can now see the basis for a system
mechanism to cause users and application programs to view the set of all files on all
machines as a single hierarchical tree. We discuss that dynamic behavior now.

3.4   Accessing the Filesystem

The important functions of the LOCUS distributed filesystem are creating and removing
objects and/or copies of objects, supporting access to and modification of those objects,
implementing atomic file update and synchronization, translating pathnames to physical
location, and providing support for remote devices and interprocess communication.
Each of these functions is examined below.

3.4.1   Logical Sites for Filesystem Activities

LOCUS is designed so that every site can be a full function node. As we saw above,
however, filesystem operations can involve more than one host. In fact there are three
logical functions in a file access and thus three logical sites. These are:

---

[1] The root or base filegroup is mounted on itself.

a. *Using site* (US), which issues the request to open a file and to which pages of the file are to be supplied.

b. *Storage site* (SS), which is the site at which a copy of the requested file is stored, and which has been selected to supply pages of that file to the using site.

c. *Current synchronization site* (CSS), which enforces a global access synchronization policy for the file's filegroup and selects SSs for each open request. A given physical site can be the CSS for any number of filegroups, but there is only one CSS for any given filegroup in any set of communicating sites (i.e., a partition). The CSS need not store any particular file in the filegroup, but in order for it to make appropriate access decisions it must have knowledge of which sites store the file and what the most current version of the file is.

There are three possible independent roles a given site can play (US, CSS, SS). A particular site can therefore operate in one of eight modes. LOCUS handles each combination, optimizing for performance.

Since all open requests for a file go through the CSS function, it is possible to implement easily a large variety of synchronization policies.

3.4.2 Synchronization

As soon as one introduces data replication, synchronization is a necessity. In addition, one must resolve how to operate when not all of the copies are accessible.

The LOCUS synchronization policy is upward compatible with the total lack of synchronization in standard Unix. In particular, the default locking policy is called *Unix mode,* which implements on multiple machines exactly what Unix has on a single machine. Processes can concurrently read and modify the same files from one or more sites. Section 3.5 describes how the single site view is maintained under these conditions.

However, LOCUS does include a distributed implementation of *lockf* - the /usr/group standard proposal for file and record synchronization. Records (byte ranges) or whole files can be locked by a process if not already locked by a different process. Locking can be advisory (only checked during the lockf call) or enforced (checked on all reads and writes). A process can chose to either fail if it cannot immediately get a lock or it can queue to wait for the bytes desired to be unlocked. Processes waiting for a lock are interruptible.

In LOCUS, so long as there is a copy of the desired resource available, it can be accessed. If there are multiple copies present, the most efficient one to access is selected. Other copies are updated in background, but the system remains responsible for supplying a mutually consistent view to the user. Within a set of communicating sites, synchronization facilities and update propagation mechanisms assure consistency of copies, as well as guaranteeing that the latest version of a file is the only one that is visible.

3.4.3   Opening and Reading Files

To read a file, a program issues the *open* system call with a filename parameter and flags indicating that the open is for read. As in standard Unix, pathname searching (or directory interrogation) is done within the operating system open call.[1] After the last directory has been interrogated, the operating system on the requesting site has a <logical filegroup number, inode number> pair for the target file that is about to be opened. If the inode information is not already in an in-core inode structure, a structure is allocated. If the file is stored locally, the local disk inode information is filled in. Otherwise very little information is initially entered.

Next, the CSS for the filegroup is interrogated. The CSS is determined by examining the logical mount table. If the local site is the CSS, only a procedure call is needed. Otherwise, a message is sent to the CSS, the CSS sets up an in-core inode for itself, calls the same procedure that would have been called if US=CSS, packages the response, and sends it back to the US. The CSS is involved for several reasons. One is to enforce synchronization controls. Enough state information is kept in core at the CSS to support those synchronization decisions. For example, if the policy allows only a single open for modification, the site where that modification is ongoing would be kept in core at the CSS. Another reason for contacting the CSS is to determine a storage site. The CSS stores a copy of the disk inode information whether or not it actually stores the file. Consequently it has a list of containers which store the file. Using that information and mount table information, the CSS can select potential storage sites. The potential sites are polled to see if they will act as storage sites.

Besides knowing the sites where the file is stored, the CSS is also responsible for knowing the latest version number. This information is passed to potential storage sites so they can check it against the version they store. If they do not yet store the latest version, they refuse to act as a storage site.

---

[1] Pathname searching is described in the next section.

Two obvious optimizations are done. First, in its message to the CSS, the US includes the version of the copy of the file it stores, if it stores the file. If that is the latest version, the CSS selects the US as the SS and just responds appropriately to the US. Another simplifying case is when the CSS stores the latest version and the US doesn't. In this case the CSS picks itself as SS (without any message overhead) and returns this information to the US.

The response from the CSS is used to complete the in-core inode information at the US. For example, if the US is not the SS then all the disk inode information (e.g., file size, ownership, permissions) is obtained from the CSS response. The CSS in turn had obtained that information from the SS. The most general open protocol (all logical functions on different physical sites) is:

US	→ CSS	OPEN request
CSS	→ SS	request for storage site
SS	→ CSS	response to previous message
CSS	→ US	response to first message.

Figure 3-6 displays this general message sequence.

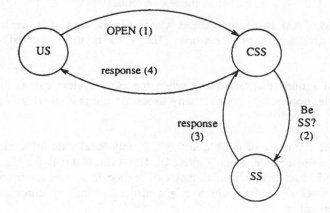

Figure 3-6: Open Protocol

After the file is open, the user-level process issues read calls. All such requests are serviced via kernel buffers, both in standard Unix and in LOCUS. In the local case data is paged from external storage devices into operating system buffers and then copied from there into the address space of the process. Access to locally stored files is the same in LOCUS as in Unix, including accessed ahead done for files being read sequentially.

Requests for data from remote sites operate similarly. Instead of allocating a buffer and queueing a request for a page from a local disk, however, the operating system at the US allocates a buffer and queues a request to be sent over the network to the SS. The request is simple. It contains the <logical filegroup, inode number> pair, the logical page number within the file, and a guess as to where the in-core inode information is stored at the SS.

At the SS, the request is treated within the operating system as follows:

a. The in-core inode is found using the guess provided.

b. The logical page number is translated into a physical disk block number.

c. A standard low-level operating system routine is called to allocate a buffer and get the appropriate page from disk (if it is not already in a buffer).

d. The buffer is queued on the network I/O queue for transmission back to the US as a response to the read request.

The protocol for a network read is thus:[1]

US	→	SS	request for page x of file y
SS	→	US	response to the above request

As in the case of local disk reads, read ahead is useful in the case of sequential behavior, both at the SS and across the network. The CSS is not involved in the I/O communication.

One of several actions can take place when the *close* system call is invoked on a remotely stored file, depending on how many times the file is concurrently open at this US.

If this is not the last close of the file at this US, only local state information need be updated (unless the open mode is being altered). However, if this is the last close of the file, the SS and CSS must be informed so they can deallocate in-core inode structures and so the CSS can alter state data which might affect its next synchronization policy decision. The protocol is:

US	→	SS	US close
SS	→	CSS	SS close
CSS	→	SS	response to above
SS	→	US	response to first message

---

[1] There are *no* other messages involved: no acknowledgements, flow control, or any other underlying mechanism. This specialized protocol is an important contributor to LOCUS performance, but it implies the need for careful higher level error handling.

Closes of course can happen as a result of error conditions like hosts crashing or network partitions. To properly effect closes at various logical sites, certain state information must be kept in the in-core inode. The US of course must know where the SS is (but then it needed that knowledge just to read pages). The CSS must know all the sites currently serving as storage sites so if a certain site crashes, the CSS can determine if a given in-core inode slot is thus no longer in use. Analogously, the SS must keep track, for each file, of all the USs that it is currently serving.

The protocols discussed here are the lowest level protocols in the system, except for some retransmission support. Because multilayered support and error handling, such as suggested by the ISO standard, is not present, much higher performance has been achieved.

3.4.4 Pathname Searching

In the previous section we outlined the protocol for opening a file given the <logical filegroup number, inode number> pair. In this section we describe how that pair is found, given a character string name.

All pathnames presented to the operating system start from one of two places, either the root (/) or the current working directory of the process presenting the pathname. In both cases an inode is in core at the US for the directory. To commence the pathname searching, the <logical filegroup, inode number> of the starting directory is extracted from the appropriate inode, and an internal open is done on it. This is the same internal open that was described at the start of the previous section, but with one difference. A directory opened for pathname searching is not open for normal READ, but instead for an internal, unsynchronized read. The distinction is that no global synchronization is done. If the directory is stored locally and there are no propagations pending to come in, the local directory is searched without informing the CSS. If the directory is not local, the protocol involving the CSS must be used, but the locking rule is such that updates to the directory can occur while interrogation is ongoing. Since no system call does more than just enter, delete, or change an entry within a directory, and since each of these actions are atomic, directory interrogation never sees an inconsistent picture.

Having opened the initial directory, protection checks are made and the directory is searched for the first pathname component. Searching of course will require reading pages of the directory, and if the directory is not stored locally these pages are read across the net in the same manner as other file data pages. If a match is found, the inode number of that component is read from the directory to continue the pathname search. The initial directory is closed (again internally), and the next component is opened. This strategy is continued up to the last component, which is opened in the manner requested by the original system call.

3.4.5 File Modification

Opening an existing file for modification is much the same as opening for read. The synchronization check at the CSS is different, and the state information kept at all three logical sites is slightly different.[1]

The act of modifying data takes on two forms. If the modification does not include the entire page, the old page is read from the SS using the read protocol. If the change involves an entire page, a buffer is set up at the US without any reads. In either case, after changes are made (possibly by delayed write), the page is eventually sent to the SS via the write protocol, which is simply:[2]

$$US \quad \rightarrow \quad SS \qquad \text{Write logical page } x \text{ in file } y$$

The action to be taken at the SS is described in the next section in the context of the commit mechanism.

The close protocol for modification is similar to the read case. However, at the US all modified pages must be flushed to the SS before the close message is sent. Also, the mechanism at the SS is again tied up with the commit mechanism, to which we now turn.

3.4.6 File Commit

The important concept of atomically committing changes has been imported from the database world and integrated into LOCUS. All changes to a given file are handled atomically. Such a commit mechanism is useful both for database work and in general, and can be integrated without performance degradation. No changes to a file are permanent until a commit operation is performed. *Commit* and *abort* (undo any changes back to the previous commit point) system calls are provided, and closing a file commits it.[3]

---

[1] Opening a file in a replicated filesystem for modification requires a little more mechanism. The primary copy of the filesystem must be available, and all processes that are currently reading this file must now use the primary copy so they will see changes immediately. This process is discussed in more detail in Section 3.7, "File Replication and Merge."

[2] There are low-level acknowledgements on this message to ensure that it is received. No higher level response is necessary.

[3] If a file is open for modification by more than one process, the changes are not made permanent until one of these process issues a commit system call or until they all close the file.

LOCUS uses a shadow page mechanism, since the advantage of logs, namely the ability to maintain strict physical relationships among data blocks, is not valuable in a Unix-style filesystem, or where record-level update does not predominate. High-performance shadowing is also easier to implement.

The US function never deals with actual disk blocks, but rather with logical pages. Thus the entire shadow page mechanism is implemented at the SS and is transparent to the US. At the SS, then, a new physical page is allocated if a change is made to an existing page of a file. This is done without any extra I/O in one of two ways: if an entire page is being changed, the new page is filled in with the new data and written to the storage medium; if the change is not of the entire page, the old page is read, the name of the buffer is changed to the new page, the changed data is entered, and this new page is written to the storage medium. Both these cases leave the old information intact. Of course it is necessary to keep track of where the old and new pages are. The disk inode contains the old page numbers. The in-core copy of the disk inode starts with the old pages, but is updated with new page numbers as shadow pages are allocated. If a given logical page is modified multiple times, it is not necessary to allocate different pages. After the first time the page is modified, it is marked as being a shadow page and reused in place for subsequent changes.

The atomic commit operation consists merely of moving the in-core inode information to the disk inode. After that point, the file permanently contains the new information. To abort a set of changes rather than commit them, one merely discards the in-core information since the old inode and pages are still on disk, and frees up those page frames on disk containing modified pages. Additional mechanism is also present to support large files that are structured through indirect pages that contain page pointers.

As is evident by the mechanism above, we have chosen to deal with file modification by first committing the change to one copy of a file, the primary copy. Because update can only happen to the primary copy of a file, changes to two different copies at the same time cannot occur blocked, and reading an old copy while another copy is being modified is avoided.[1] As part of the commit operation, the SS sends messages to all the other SSs of that file as well as the CSS. At a minimum, these messages identify the file and contain the new version number. Additionally, for performance reasons, the message can indicate: (a) whether it was just inode information that changed and no data (e.g., ownership or permissions) or (b) which explicit logical pages were modified. At this

---

[1] Simultaneous read and modification at different sites are allowed for directory files as described earlier. This action enhances performance significantly. The other storage sites for the directory learn of the new version by normal means, so that subsequent nolock directory reads at those sites will see the updated version. A site that doesn't store the directory, but is using nolock read for the directory, and thus perhaps has the (old) directory page in its buffer cache, is notified of the new version by its storage site.

point it is the responsibility of these additional SSs to bring their version of the file up-to-date by propagating in the entire file or just the changes. A queue of propagation requests is kept within the kernel at each site and a kernel process services the queue.

Propagation is done by "pulling" the data rather than "pushing" it. The propagation process which wants to page over changes to a file first internally opens the file at a site which has the latest version. It then issues standard read messages either for all the pages or just the modified ones. When each page arrives, the buffer that contains it is renamed and sent out to secondary storage, thus avoiding copying data into and out of an application data space, as would be necessary if this propagation mechanism were to run as an application-level process. Note also that this propagation-in procedure uses the standard commit mechanism, so if contact is lost with the site containing the newer version, the local site is left with a coherent, complete copy of the file, albeit still out of date.

Given this commit mechanism, one is always left with either the original file or a completely changed file, but never with a partially made change, even in the face of local or foreign site failures. Such was not the case in the standard Unix environment.

3.5 Synchronizing Distributed Filesystem Activity

In standard Unix, multiple processes are permitted to have the same file open concurrently. These processes issue read and write system calls and the system guarantees that each successive operation sees the effects of the ones that precede it. This is implemented fairly easily by having the processes access the same operating system data structures and data cache, and by using locks on data structures to serialize requests.

In the multiple site environment in which LOCUS operates, concurrent file activity could be supported in a number of ways. One could keep all data related to a file at one site, a single SS. In this approach, read and write requests from application programs would be passed directly to the SS and the data would be copied directly between the SS and the application process. There would be no local caching at the US of the file length, content, or current position within the file, since these values may be changed by processes at other sites.

A second approach would be to enforce an exclusive writer, shared reader model which, at any point in time, permitted either one process (or multiple processes on a single site) to have a file open for write with no processes on other sites permitted to read the file, or multiple processes to have a file open for read with no writing processes. This would allow caching of data at remote using sites while the file was open, since the system would guarantee that no process on another site could modify the file. This approach, while performing better than the first by caching data closer to the processes that need it, must be rejected because it is not Unix. Unix permits multiple processes to hold the same file open for write and so must any solution LOCUS employs.

The approach adopted by LOCUS is to permit an arbitrary assortment of reading and writing processes on various sites in the network. Information about the file will be cached at each US, but the cached information may be marked invalid at certain points in time as the file is actively being modified by processes on other sites. A *token* mechanism has been employed to ensure that cached information is kept up-to-date. This mechanism is discussed in the following subsections.

3.5.1   Open Files in Unix

As in standard Unix, four levels of LOCUS data structures are used to record system information about open files. These data structures are maintained by the operating system on behalf of the application processes; and in the network environment in which LOCUS operates, some of them must be shared among processes executing on different sites. A significant amount of effort has gone into the design of LOCUS to synchronize access to these distributed data structures in an efficient manner. But, before embarking on a description of the LOCUS data structures, let us take a brief look at how they are used in standard Unix. See Figures 3-7a and 3-7b. The LOCUS data structures extend these to handle additional function (such as the file commit mechanism discussed earlier) and to support distributed operation.

Each application process in Unix refers to open files using a small, nonnegative integer, called a *file descriptor*. The file descriptor is used as an index into the first data structure, the per-process open file array. This array is used to map process file descriptors to entries in a system-wide pool of *file offset* structures.[1]

The file offset structure, the second level of data structures, holds the *file offset*, the current offset into the file which is used when reading or writing a file sequentially. Also in this structure are flags indicating the mode (read, write, read/write) under which this file was opened. One of these file offset structures is allocated by each *open* or *create* system call.[2] A single file offset structure can be referred to by several file descriptors in one of two ways. First, a single process may obtain two file descriptors which refer to

---

[1] This data structure is often referred to as a *file block*, not to be confused with the data pages of a file.

[2] Two are created by the *pipe* system call, one for the read end of the pipe and one for the write end.

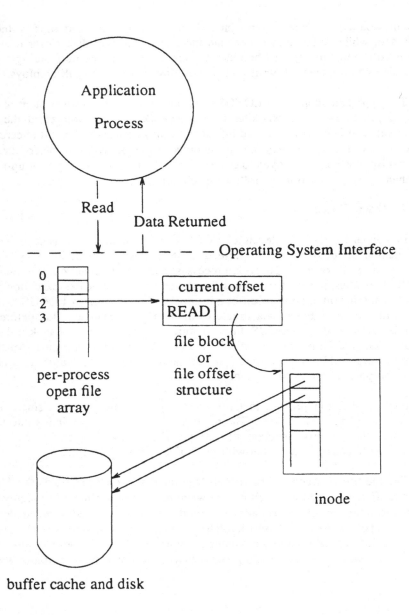

Figure 3-7a: Data Structures For an Open File in Unix

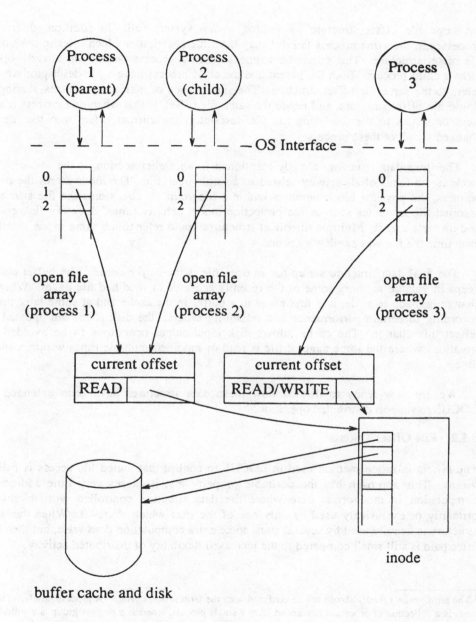

Figure 3-7b: File Open by more than One Process in Unix

the same file offset structure by issuing a *dup* system call. In addition, different processes in the same process family[1] may have file descriptors which refer to the same file offset structure. This condition happens when a process with a file already open forks a child process. Both the parent and the child process have a file descriptor which refers to the same file offset structure. The significance of multiple processes sharing a single file offset structure, and hence the same file offset, is that when one process reads from or writes to the file using his file descriptor, the current offset into the file is changed for all of these processes.

The third data structure, already mentioned in an earlier section, is the *inode*. The inode is the focus of all activity related to a single open file. The inode stores the page pointers, the physical block numbers within a filegroup. It also stores the file size and assorted file attributes such as file protection mode, activity times, directory link count and owner's userid. Multiple file offset structures could refer to the same inode, one for each time the file was explicitly opened.

The final data structure set up for an open file is the *buffer cache*. The buffer cache keeps in volatile memory some of the recently accessed or modified file pages. When a change is made to a file, it is first made to a buffer in the cache and at some later time, according to certain performance and reliability criteria, the disk pages are updated to reflect this change. The cache allows disk input/output operations to be avoided in situations where the same page of file is read or modified multiple times within a short time.

We are now ready to discuss how these data structures have been extended in LOCUS to support distributed operation.

3.5.2 File Offset Tokens

The synchronization method used in LOCUS to control distributed file access is called *tokens*. This approach has the desirable property that it causes very little additional computation in the normal case where the data structure controlled with tokens is primarily or exclusively used by only one of the sites which shares it. When the data structure is heavily used by several sites, some extra computation does arise, but then the price paid is still small compared to the increased flexibility of distributed activity.

---

[1] The term *process family* should not be confused with the term *process group*. A process family, as used here, is a collection of processes descended from a single process, whereas a process group is a collection of processes which are functioning together in some way and which it makes sense to signal and otherwise control as a group. The assignment of processes to process groups is done according to conventions imposed by application programs such as command shells.

A *file offset token* allows a file offset structure to be shared between processes on multiple sites.[1] The file offset structure includes the file offset and some status fields. The presence or absence of the token is indicated in one of the status fields. Unix allows a file offset structure to be shared between multiple processes in the same process family. LOCUS extends this sharing to allow processes in the same family to reside on different machines in the network.[2] When a file offset structure is shared among multiple sites, only the site which has the file offset token for this structure is guaranteed to have an up-to-date file offset. Other sites must first acquire the offset token (and the current file offset) from this site before accessing the file. See Figure 3-8.

A single site, the *token manager site,* controls the allocation of the file offset token. This site is typically the SS for the open file, but it may be a different site if the SS for the file changes while the file is open.[3] The token manager site and the various using sites which share the offset structure interact using messages. A using site may send a message to the token manager site requesting the offset token. If the offset token is not already assigned at the time a request arrives, the token manager site sends a message back to the using site granting it the token. If the token has already been assigned to another using site when the request arrives, the token manager site sends a message to the current token site, attempting to recall the token. That using site completes operations already in progress, if any, and then sends a message back to the token manager site, releasing the token. At that time, the token can be assigned to the waiting process.

If multiple sites request the offset token at the same time, the requests are queued at the token manager site, and the token is assigned to each site in turn. A using site, upon receiving the token, is notified if another site is waiting to receive the token and thus behaves as though the token manager site attempted to recall the token immediately after it was granted. The using site, therefore, performs those actions that were suspended, awaiting the arrival of the token, and then releases the token back to the token manager site, and hence to the next using site in the queue.

More than one process on a single site may be sharing a file offset structure. Since the offset token is assigned to a site rather than to a single process, each of these processes may make use of the shared file offset while the token is present. Special care is given in LOCUS so that multiple processes can make use of the file offset while the

---

[1] File Offset Tokens and the File Offset Structure are also referred to as the Offset Token and Offset Structure in this book.

[2] See the description of remote tasking functions in Chapter 4.

[3] The SS for an open file may change if a replicated file open for read by one process is later opened for write by another process. At this time, all opens for read must be changed to use the same SS, in order for all processes to see changes immediately.

Using Site	Token Manager Site	Using Site 2
US1	TMS	US2

Assume the file offset token for this shared file offset structure is held by using site 1. If the process on using site 2 issues a *Read* system call, the file offset token must be acquired first, so a message requesting the token is sent to the Token Manager Site.

$$\text{TMS} \xleftarrow{\quad\text{RQSTOK}\quad} \text{US2}$$

Since the token is held by another site it must be recalled from that site. A "release token" message is sent

$$\text{US1} \xleftarrow{\quad\text{RELTOK}\quad} \text{TMS}$$

If no operation using the file offset is in progress, the token will be released immediately. If an operation is in progress, the token will be released when the current operation completes. The "token released" message announces that the token is being released and specifies the current file offset

$$\text{US1} \xrightarrow{\quad\text{TOKRLSD (file offset)}\quad} \text{TMS}$$

Now the TMS can grant the token to site 2.

$$\text{TMS} \xrightarrow{\quad\text{AWARDTOK (file offset)}\quad} \text{US2}$$

At this point, using site 2 has the file offset token and the most recent value of the file offset. It may then proceed with the *Read* system call. Subsequent *Read* system calls will notice the presence of the token, avoid the above protocol for acquiring the token, and proceed immediately with normal *Read* system call actions.

Figure 3-8: Network Messages For Acquiring File Offset Token

token is present, while at the same time sites are prevented from usurping the token indefinitely. The first process on a site to notice that the file offset token is not held sends a message to the token manager site requesting the token. While awaiting the arrival of the token, this process marks the file offset structure so that other processes will not send duplicate requests, but instead they will join the first process in awaiting the token's arrival. After the token arrives, all processes waiting for it continue the system call they were performing. System calls issued by processes on the same site while the token is held are permitted to run immediately. At some point the token manager site may recall the token in order to grant it to another site. If the token cannot be released immediately because a system call in progress is using the file offset, the file offset structure is marked as *wanted*. When this happens, no new system calls using this file offset are permitted to begin, the in-progress system calls eventually finish, and as the last one finishes, it releases the token. If newly initiated system calls are suspended because the token was wanted by the token manager site, the token is re-requested at this time.

Thus, file offset tokens provide an efficient means to share a file offset structure between processes on multiple using sites. One of the disadvantages of this approach, it should be noted, is that since the file offset is stored at only the site which has the file offset token, the loss of that site may cause the current value of the file offset to be lost. Processes on other sites which share the same file offset structure must use an out-of-date value of the file offset, rereading the same portion of a file, for example. Another possible disadvantage of the token approach is that the token manager site may end up being a site not otherwise involved with the open file. This condition presents the possibility of additional failure modes, since correct operation now depends on the token manager site remaining operational.

3.5.3 File Data Tokens

Another data structure which can be shared between multiple sites is the (using site) inode. *File Data tokens* are used to synchronize shared inodes.[1] As with standard Unix, inodes can be shared between multiple processes either because two or more processes opened the file independently, in which case each process uses a separate file offset, or because two or more processes in the same process family share the same file offset and in so doing also share the inode. Data tokens are used in both of these cases when the processes happen to reside on two or more different sites throughout the network. Unlike offset tokens, there are two types of data tokens: *read* tokens and *write* tokens. These data tokens are assigned to sites using the policy that at most one site at a time may hold a write token for a given file. The presence or absence of the read and write data tokens is kept in a status field in the inode. Multiple sites, however, may each hold a read token if no other site holds a write token for the file. Only a site with the write token may

---

[1] File Data Tokens will be referred to simply as Data Tokens.

modify a file's content.[1] Any site with a read token may read a file's content. With this multiple reader, single writer semantics, file synchronization reduces to the simpler synchronization method outlined before. The primary complication is in managing the recalling of the data tokens from sites while at the same time maintaining fair scheduling so that no site can usurp the token.

The data buffer is a third data structure which is shared between multiple sites. The buffer cache holds the actual data pages of the file (the file content) at each using site. These buffers are guaranteed to contain valid information only when the file's data token is present and as such might logically be considered an extension of the file's inode. When the write data token is taken from a site, the inode is copied back to the SS, as are all modified data pages. When an data token is granted to a site, the inode is copied from the SS, but data pages cannot easily be updated. Since arbitrary changes may have occurred to the file while the token was not present, all cached buffers are invalidated when the token is released.

Thus, the presence of an data token at a using site for a file indicates that the file length and content may be trusted. The method for requesting, granting, recalling and releasing the data token is much the same as for file offset tokens. The token manager site for data tokens is the SS for the open file. The major difference is that the token manager site may grant multiple read tokens to sites at one time, and when a site requests the write tokens, all of the read tokens must be recalled instead of just recalling a single file offset token.

Operations such as *stat* (examine file attributes), *link* (make an additional directory entry for the file) and *chmod* (change the access controlling information associated with the file), which examine or change certain file attributes, do not require the use of data tokens. Data tokens are not required because changes to these file attributes, like changes to the contents of a directory, may only occur completely within atomic system calls whose explicit purpose is to change these attributes.[2] LOCUS, therefore, sends these requests to change file attributes directly to the SS where the change can be made, committed, and propagated to all storage and using sites according to the normal update propagation method.

---

[1] Except for directories, where updates are made within a single system call and then propagated to all storage and using sites immediately. The special treatment of directories is called for by the requirement that searching local directories be efficient and not require synchronization with the CSS.

[2] The exception to this statement is that the file length *is* controlled by the data token, and not acquiring the token when doing a stat system call may cause users or programs to discern out-of-date file length information on an open file. LOCUS may need to be extended in the future so that applications may find out length information on open files.

To see how offset tokens and data tokens work together, consider a write system call invocation. First, the file offset token is obtained and locked in such a way that it is guaranteed to be held throughout the write operation. Next, the data token is obtained and similarly locked. The tokens are always acquired and locked in this order to avoid deadlocks. The lock, in each case, is a count of the number of processes with operations in progress. When the operation is finished, the two token locks are removed, and if this is the last unlock for one of the tokens and that token had been requested by another site, the file offset structure or the inode will be marked accordingly, and the token will then be released back to the appropriate token manager site.

To summarize, LOCUS allows files to be held open concurrently by multiple processes. Application programs and users see the same system behavior whether they run programs all on one site or split across several sites, and the behavior they see is the same behavior they would have seen under standard Unix. File offset tokens are used when two or more processes on different sites have file descriptors referring to the same file offset. This can happen as the result of a process spawning a child or an entire family of processes while it held a file open, thus causing the open file to be inherited by the other processes. Data tokens allow a process at one site to see the changes made to a file at another site. Only changes to the actual content of the file, including the file length, is controlled by data tokens. Changes to other file attributes, such as owner and access protection mode, are effected at the SS and propagated to other sites without making use of file offset or data tokens. The token mechanism employed here only adds significant system overhead when the degree of sharing between sites is high, and even in that case, this approach performs acceptably and fairly.

3.6   Filesystem Support for Interprocess Communication

Pipes are a Unix facility by which data may be passed conveniently among programs. In order to maintain a high degree of transparency in LOCUS, it is necessary that pipes between processes on different sites operate with exactly the same effect as local pipes. LOCUS supports named and unnamed pipes in a manner completely transparent to the user. Together with the facilities available to control the execution site of processes, this transparent pipe facility helps make it straightforward to execute multiple-process programs in a distributed way, even when they were originally written for a traditional single-site Unix environment. In addition, network transparent pipes are a convenient facility for more general data exchange.

In the following sections, the functionality of Unix pipes is briefly reviewed, and the LOCUS architecture for network transparent pipes is presented.

3.6.1 Pipe Semantics

A pipe is a one-way communication mechanism between programs. The output of one or more programs is directed to the input of one or more other programs through a pipe. No intermediate file is necessary. The pipe is a first-in, first-out stream of bytes. Once data has been successfully written to the pipe, no significance is assigned to the boundary between individual write requests. There is no out-of-band or in-band signaling mechanism, or any data-typing present, except that which might be imposed by a higher level mechanism. The implementation must ensure that all data written on the write end of a pipe can be read, in the proper order, from the read end of the pipe.

The pipe is a finite length buffer which can hold at least 10,240 bytes of data. An attempt to read data from an empty pipe, one in which all data written has already been read, causes the reading process to block, waiting for more data to be written into the pipe. This is a principal difference between pipes and regular files, where an end-of-file indication would have been returned in this situation. Attempting to read more data from the pipe than has been written returns that portion that is available, even though it is less than the amount requested. Again, this cannot happen for regular files unless the reader is at the end of a file or there is an active process writing to the file as well. An attempt to read data from a pipe after all of the writers have gone away and after all data has been drained from the pipe causes the reader to receive an end-of-file indication.

An attempt to write more data than will fit in the pipe, i.e., an amount that causes the amount of unread data to exceed the length of the pipe, causes the writing process to block, waiting for enough data to be read from the pipe to allow the attempted write system call to succeed. Thus, write requests of a length up to the length of the pipe are atomic in that either all or none of the supplied data is ever added to the pipe. It is not possible for only part of the supplied data to be written or for the reader to be given only the first part of a single write request unless the reader was given exactly the amount of data that was requested. An attempt to write data on a pipe after all readers have gone away causes the writer to receive the SIGPIPE signal. The writing process may elect to catch this signal and carry on with the rest of its code, or it may elect to take the default action for this signal, which is to terminate execution.

A reader, waiting on an empty pipe, or a writer, waiting on a full pipe, may each be interrupted. If they are interrupted, no data will have been transferred to or from the pipe, and the state of the pipe will be as though the read or write system call had not been issued.

Pipes are set up in one of two ways. Traditional pipes are created using the *pipe* system call. This system call creates an empty pipe and returns back to the application process a read and a write file descriptor. By using the *fork* system call, this initial process can spawn an entire family of processes. One or more of these processes will keep the (inherited) read file descriptor open, while one or more of the other processes will keep the write file descriptor open. These process use the *write* and *read* system calls to transfer data to or from the pipe, and use the *close* system call when data transfer is completed. This type of pipe is also called an *unnamed* pipe, in contrast with the other type of pipe, a *named* pipe, which actually has a name entered in a filesystem directory. These named pipes are opened using the standard *open* system call. One or more processes may open the pipe specifying an open mode of *read*, while one or more other processes may open the pipe specifying an open mode of *write*. After at least one reader and writer have opened the named pipe, it behaves exactly like the unnamed one, except now the collection of communicating processes is not limited to being in the same process family, but instead may by arbitrary processes in the system. Also, after all readers and writers have closed the pipe, the pipe is not deleted, but remains in the filesystem as an empty pipe ready to be opened by another collection of communicating processes.

3.6.2   Network Transparent Pipes in LOCUS

The basic architectural model for pipes in LOCUS has three sites: the current reading site (RS), the current writing site (WS), and the storage site (SS).[1] The RS and WS are each using sites, but it becomes useful to differentiate them when discussing the roles each site plays. The SS is a natural centralized point, and consequently has been chosen as the site to control the pipe. For an unnamed pipe, the SS is typically the site on which the *pipe* system call was issued. For a named pipe the SS is the site that stores the filegroup in which it is named.[2]

The basic flow is that the WS sends data to the SS and the RS requests data from the SS using the standard LOCUS read and write network messages used for accessing ordinary files. See Figure 3-9 for the general message exchange. The SS keeps track of the data which is in the pipe and controls the blocking and unblocking of the reader and

---

[1] This is the most general case, of course. In fact, quite often two or three of these roles would be co-located on the same site, thus simplifying the algorithm and reducing the amount of multisite synchronization necessary. Later in this chapter we discuss the treatment of multiple reading and writing sites, a case which is handled by considering only one of the reading sites and one of the writing sites as current at any point in time.

[2] In the event the filegroup is replicated, the pipe is not really replicated. Only the primary copy can be modified, so it serves as the SS. Data pages are never committed, so the only information ever propagated to other copies of the filegroup is inode information such as activity times and protection mode.

writer. When the reader or writer is at the SS, their behavior is very much the same as in standard Unix. Reader blocking on empty pipe and writer blocking on full pipe is determined by the same conditions. Only the case when the reader or writer is not at the SS requires elaboration here.

In the most general, three-site case, each site keeps track of the data it knows to be in the pipe, even though at any given point in time the sites may not be in agreement with one another. This potential disagreement is because the sites' only means of communication is via network messages such as read, write, and others discussed below. It is when these messages arrive that the RS, WS, and SS learn what activity has taken place at the other sites, and at this time that each site refines its knowledge as to the amount of data still in the pipe. The RS and WS act according to their view of the pipe and consult the SS when necessary.

For example, when the RS notices what it thinks is an empty pipe, it attempts to read the next page of data from the SS anyway. If data had arrived at the SS recently, the SS would be able to satisfy the read request, the RS would be informed how much data the SS knows to be in the pipe, and the RS could then return the appropriate data to the waiting application process. Only if the SS also believed the pipe to be empty would special processing be required. In this case, the SS either informs the RS that end-of-file has been reached because no writer holds the pipe open any longer, or informs the RS that the reading process should go to sleep because there is no data available to be read yet. In the latter case, the SS would remember that he told the reader to sleep, and would later send a *reader wakeup* message to the RS. Upon receipt of this message the RS would reissue the read message and either receive the data it wanted or be informed now of the end-of-file condition. When the SS received the read message from the RS, it was able to infer some information about how far the reader had read. The SS learned that all data *before* this requested page of data had been read. It doesn't know how much of the new page, if any, will be consumed by the reader, and so makes no assumption about that.

The WS follows a similar approach. As the application process issues write system calls to write data to the pipe, the same data is immediately sent via write messages to the SS. As the SS may have more recent information about the amount of data in the pipe, the WS disregards its own idea and trusts the SS to tell it when to stop.[1] The standard approach for reporting errors to a process writing data from a remote using site is used here for informing the WS that the all readers had gone away.

---

[1] The precise mechanism for stopping the writer is related to the use of file offset tokens.

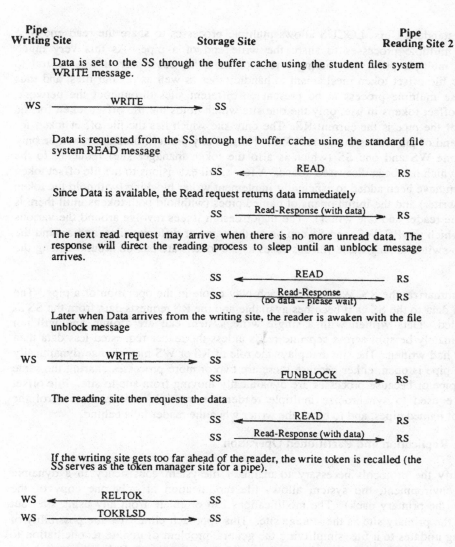

Pipe Writing Site   **Storage Site**   **Pipe Reading Site 2**

Data is set to the SS through the buffer cache using the student files system WRITE message.

WS ——————WRITE——————▶ SS

Data is requested from the SS through the buffer cache using the standard file system READ message

SS ◀——————READ—————— RS

Since Data is available, the Read request returns data immediately

SS ——Read-Response (with data)——▶ RS

The next read request may arrive when there is no more unread data. The response will direct the reading process to sleep until an unblock message arrives.

SS ◀——————READ—————— RS
SS ——Read-Response (no data -- please wait)——▶ RS

Later when Data arrives from the writing site, the reader is awaken with the file unblock message

WS ——————WRITE——————▶ SS
SS ——————FUNBLOCK—————▶ RS

The reading site then requests the data

SS ◀——————READ—————— RS
SS ——Read-Response (with data)——▶ RS

If the writing site gets too far ahead of the reader, the write token is recalled (the SS serves as the token manager site for a pipe).

WS ◀——————RELTOK—————— SS
WS ——————TOKRLSD—————▶ SS

The write token will not be granted to any site until the reader consumes enough of the data in the pipe.

Figure 3-9: Network Messages For Pipes -- General 3-Site Case

As in standard Unix, LOCUS allows multiple processes to share the read end of a pipe and multiple processes to share the write end of a pipe. As this very much resembles multiple processes sharing a read or write file descriptor, it was natural to extend the file offset token mechanism to handle pipes as well as regular files, and thus allow those multiple process to be present on different sites throughout the network. With file offset tokens in use, only the one site which holds the file offset token for the read end of the pipe is the current RS. The only site which has the file offset token for the write end of the pipe is the current WS. Thus, at any point in time there will be only one RS, one WS and one SS (which is also the token manager site) reducing to the situation which has been discussed above. A few small extensions to the file offset token mechanism have been added to efficiently implement writer blocking (withhold the token from the writer) and the initial opens of named pipes (withhold both tokens until there is at least one reader and one writer). The major design issues revolve around the various ways in which the RS, WS, and SS can be on the same or different sites, and around the method to switch among these various cases as the tokens are passed around among the sites.

To summarize, the RS, WS, and SS each play a role in the operation of a pipe. The WS sends data to the SS as it becomes available and the RS requests data from the SS as it is needed. Data written with a single write system call are atomic and will not indiscriminately be split across separate reads unless the reader requested less data than the writer had written. The site that plays the role of RS or WS may change dynamically while the pipe is open, either because there are two or more processes sharing the same end of a pipe or because processes are dynamically moving from site to site. File offset tokens are used to synchronize multiple readers or multiple writers, to control the opening of named pipes, and to block the writer when the reader falls behind.

3.7 File Replication and Partitioned Operation

To simplify the protocols necessary to maintain filesystem consistency in a dynamic network environment, the system allows file modification at only one copy of the filegroup (the primary pack). The modifications can originate from any using site, but must use the primary site as the storage site. This approach eliminates the possibility of conflicting updates to a file, simplifying the general problem of update reconciliation to one of update detection and propagation. While this approach limits availability somewhat (the primary pack must be in the user's partition for a file to be modified), it works well for filegroups like the system root, where updates are rare and universal readability essential. The commit and update propagation protocols keep the packs synchronized during normal operation.

The system attempts to maintain file access across partition changes. If it is possible without loss of information to substitute a different copy of a file for one lost because of partition, the system will do so. In particular, if a process loses contact with a file it was reading remotely, the system will attempt to reopen a different copy of the same version of the file.

3.7.1 Update Detection and Propagation in a Partitioned Environment

As files are modified, the modifications propagate to the secondary packs, maintaining a globally consistent filesystem. If, however, the system partitions, making one or more of the secondary packs unavailable, those packs may be out-of-date when communication resumes, and the system must take extraordinary measures to synchronize them. Doing so efficiently requires keeping additional information during normal operation so that the overhead to detect and propagate changes is minimized.

To this end, the system maintains a sequence number (the commit count) for each filegroup, enumerating each commit to any file. The current sequence number is kept in the superblock and as any file is committed, that sequence number is stored in the inode of the committed file and the sequence number is incremented. As a result, each inode has a record of when it was last updated with respect to all other files in the filegroup. The commit count is used by the system in many ways to eliminate or reduce costly searches and comparisons. In addition, the system maintains, for each pack, a low-water-mark (lwm), a high-water-mark (hwm) and a list of recent commits. The lwm represents a point of synchronization: the system guarantees that all relevant commits done prior to the lwm have been propagated to the pack. The hwm records the most recent change to any file that the pack knows about, whether it has propagated the change or not. At the primary site, the lwm always equals the hwm. The list of recent commits is discussed below.

Whenever the lwm on a pack equals or exceeds the hwm on another pack, the system knows that no updates need to be propagated from the second pack to the first. When the system suspects that a pack is inconsistent, it brings it up to date by propagating the files that have changed, determined by one of two mechanisms: the first, a simple, low-overhead kernel protocol that handles only a limited number of changes; the second, a more general application process that has greater overhead but can reconcile the entire filesystem.

3.7.1.1 Kernel Based Reconciliation

During normal operation, the system keeps a list of the most recent commits in the superblock of the file pack. Whenever a commit occurs at a storage site, the inode number and the commit count are recorded in the list. At the primary site this results in a complete list of the most recent commits; at other storage sites the list may have some holes. When a pack joins a partition and its lwm is within the range of the list, it immediately schedules propagations on the listed files, and the normal operation protocols bring the pack into consistency.

If the primary pack is not available, the system will choose some other site as the CSS. If that site has not propagated all the latest changes, it will attempt to do so from other sites before servicing CSS requests. Consequently all sites always see the latest version of a file available. After the CSS has propagated all the latest commits it can finish, other sites can reconcile themselves with this CSS. Since the CSS may not have all the latest commits, other sites may also remain slightly behind the primary site until that site is again on the network. It is always the case, however, that all communicating sites see the same view of the filegroup and that view is as complete as possible given the sites that are currently part of the network.

3.7.1.2 Application Level Reconciliation Process

When a filegroup is too far out-of-date for the kernel reconciliation procedure to handle, the system invokes an application-level process to reconcile the filegroup. At this point, the system lacks sufficient knowledge of the most recent commits to replay the modifications, but must instead inspect the entire inode space to determine which files to propagate. Only after it has completed this exhaustive search can it be certain of consistency, and only after propagation is complete can it adjust its lwm to that of the remote pack.

The appliation level reconciliation process (AR) considers only a single pair of storage sites. Each site has a AR master process running which forks a child to reconcile a particular filegroup. For most sites, the packs chosen to be reconciled are the local pack and the CSS pack. In partitions lacking a primary site, the CSS first reconciles itself with the most current available pack before the other sites reconcile themselves with the CSS.

3.7.2   Replicated Copy Control

In general, a site does not need to store all of the files in a given filesystem. The root filesystem in a heterogeneous environment, for example, must contain load modules for all machines types, but a machine of type A may have no reason to store a load module for a machine of type B. A user filesystem with primary storage on a mainframe and secondary copies scattered through a number of workstations might contain files for several users, but a user on one workstation should not need to store the other users' files. Clearly, the system must provide facilities to control storage at the file level.

LOCUS has three types of file packs: primary, backbone, and secondary. Primary packs have already been discussed at length; they must store all files in the filegroup. Backbone packs are the preferred sites to act as CSS when the primary site is unavailable and can be used by other sites to reconcile in the absence of the primary pack. They also store all files. These types are both intended to improve system behavior and are maintained by the system. Secondary packs, on the other hand, store only those files required by the local site. A particular file will only be stored at a site if some user action has been taken requesting the storage.

One method available to the user is to make an explicit request for the file at a site. The request must be repeated on every site where storage is desired. This interface allows a user to store an entire directory subtree locally, but he would have to pull newly created files across to the local site periodically to maintain the tree because there is no provision for the system to do this automatically. One obvious way to use this mechanism is to set up a program to be executed at logout to bring over all newly created files in the user's home directory tree to his personal workstation.

This method is poorly suited for system administration functions, however. Creating a new file and storing it on a set of sites is difficult, particularly when not all of the sites are available. A second storage mechanism allows a user to give a file a set of storage attributes which the system compares with the attributes of the file packs to determine whether to store a particular file. This makes it easy, for example, to create a new load module and store it at all machines of that type.

The two mechanisms complement each other well. The first allows file storage control based on the hierarchical structure of the filesystem, while the second allows control based on the properties of the file itself.

3.8   High Performance

The LOCUS architecture has been carefully designed to provide high performance. LOCUS performs as well as or better than comparable Unix systems when run in a single-machine environment or when accessing local resources in a multi-machine system. In addition, LOCUS performs almost as well when accessing remote resources. Achieving these high levels of performance has been accomplished through a variety of methods.

3.8.1   Special-Case Code

It is important that local operations not be degraded in performance because of the existence of the mechanisms for access to remote resources. Many systems have succumbed to this phenomenon. LOCUS achieves its high local performance, in part, by containing special code for the local resource cases. Tests are performed early in processing and the special case code is used, bypassing more extensive portions of the general remote access software.

As an example, while the system contains code to handle the possibility that each of the various sites needed to access a file (the using, storage, and synchronization sites) are disjoint, it is quite common for two or possibly all three to be co-located. In that case, the general algorithm is not used, and special-case shortcuts are employed. As another example, when searching directories, the system attempts to use local directories without contacting the synchronization site when the local directory is up to date.

3.8.2   High-Performance Algorithms

Many of the algorithms in LOCUS have been specifically chosen to provide high performance. For example, the single file commit mechanism, described earlier, uses an intentions list strategy that requires no additional disk I/O operations. A critical issue in network performance involves the number of messages sent and the cost in processing a message. Many systems utilize complex layered protocols involving many messages in order to deal with the errors, flow control, congestion, and other issues which arise in long-haul networks. The protocols are complex enough that the processing required is also significant, often involving process and other context switches.

LOCUS is designed with the assumption that much of the time it is operating in a local network environment. These networks are characterized by relatively high bandwidth (1 megabit or higher), low delay, and virtually error-free communications. Interfaces are increasingly being designed with multimessage buffers so that back-to-back messages can be received without the requirement of an interrupt having been processed to reprime the interface. In this environment, minimizing the message costs is essential. LOCUS does so partly by the use of special-purpose protocols designed specifically for the kernel-to-kernel communication which predominates. For example, normally the read function sends a request for the desired block of a file. The data block is returned directly. No acknowledgment or other messages are sent. By careful optimization of these case-specific or *problem-oriented protocols,* significant performance gains occur.

Because the protocols have been simplified, LOCUS is also able to minimize the protocol and message processing overhead by performing much of the processing at interrupt level, rather than in a user process. In those cases where the protocol requires more complex service, a special kernel server process handles the message. These kernel processes execute in kernel address space and require very little overhead to invoke compared with a normal user process.

If necessary, the LOCUS protocols may be encapsulated in other protocols by opening a channel between communicating LOCUS kernels, so long as there is a high-performance datagram service supplied by that protocol.

3.8.3 Networks of Fast and Slow Systems

A typical LOCUS network might have many relatively slow machines, such as small personal computers, and fewer high-performance large mainframes. It is important that the system be designed so that the high-performance machines are not delayed by the lower performance ones. Several design choices in LOCUS were made taking this notion into consideration. For example, normally file replication is performed in the background after file commit, so that the large mainframe can continue the user's computation rather than waiting for the propagation of the replicated file.

3.8.4 Optimization Control

LOCUS transparency largely hides the existence of the network from users and application programs such that (in most cases) they need not even be aware of the network. However, there are cases where the user desires to "see through" the transparency and take actions based on knowledge of the underlying network. The most common case is for optimization. LOCUS provides several facilities which allow the user to make such optimization controls.

First, within the limits allowed by the system administrators, the user has the option of controlling both the number and locations of copies of replicated files and can dynamically change those decisions.

Second, a sophisticated mechanism is provided so that the user can control (within dynamically alterable limits) the machines on which processes are executed. The mechanism allows the specification of a preferred list of machines to be used when a command is to be executed.

Finally, when necessary, the user can base decisions on the dynamic behavior of the system. Information available includes the locations of files to be used, the load on the various machines, and even the amount of free disk space available on the various disks in the network.

3.9   Gateways

The LOCUS architecture functions best in a high-speed, low-delay, low-error-rate network environment. Often it will be the case that all LOCUS sites are on the same communication medium so all sites can directly communicate with all other sites. However, there are also several reasons why one would have gateways on a LOCUS network.

First, one may have more than one physical LAN. For example, one may have two differing technologies (e.g., ring and Ethernet). Alternatively, the bandwidth of network communications may necessitate more than one physical network. In either case a gateway between the physical networks would be needed.

Another reason for a gateway is that sites are physically distributed. One could have a satellite or phone link joining two parts of a network. At each end of this kind of link there could be a gateway.

The initial LOCUS architecture for the gateway function is quite straightforward. Routing is static, with each site storing for each destination site, a site to which messages should be sent for forwarding. The packet header, then, must contain four sites: the originator, the immediate sender, the immediate destination, and the final destination. A dynamic routing facility can be added as an extension in user code; it will update the final destination/immediate destination tables.

The gateway site does the forwarding in a simple fashion in the kernel. When a message is received whose final destination site is not the local site, the site fields are adjusted and the message is queued on the appropriate network. No application code is necessary and the amount of kernel code is quite small.

In the face of multihop packet traversal, there are two choices for how to acknowledge those messages needing acknowledgments. One can either do end-to-end or link-level acknowledgments. Neither strategy is difficult to implement. End-to-end acknowledgements are currently being used.

3.10 Other Issues

The LOCUS name service implemented by the directory system is also used to support remote device access, as well as to aid in handling heterogeneous machine types in a transparent manner. We turn to these issues now.

3.10.1 Files Specific to a Machine Type

Globally unique, user-visible file naming is of course very important. However, occasionally there are situations where a filename must be interpreted specially, based on the context in which it was issued. *Machine-type* context is a good example. In a LOCUS net containing both Motorola M68000s and DEC VAX 750s, for example, a user would wish to type the same command name on either type of machine and get the same service. However, the load modules of the programs providing that service could not be identical and would thus have to have different globally unique names. To get the proper load modules executed when the user types a command requires use of the machine-type context as part of name translation. A discussion of transparency and the context issue was given in Chapter 2. Here we outline a mechanism implemented in LOCUS which allows context sensitive files to be named and accessed transparently.

The scheme consists of four parts:

a. Make the globally unique name of the object in question refer to a special kind of directory (hereafter referred to as a *hidden directory)* instead of the object itself.

b. Inside this directory put the different versions of the file, naming them based on the context with which they are associated. For example, have the command name */bin/who* be a hidden directory with the file entries *68K* and *VAX* that are the respective load modules.

c. Keep a per-process inherited context for these hidden directories. If a hidden directory is found at the end of pathname searching (see Section 3.4.4 for pathname searching), it is examined for a match with the process's context rather than the next component of the pathname passed to the system.

d. Give users and programs an escape mechanism to make hidden directories visible so they can be examined and specific entries manipulated.

This scheme is discussed again in Chapter 6, Heterogeneity.

3.10.2   Files Specific to a Given Site

There are a few files and subtrees often stored in a Unix "root" filesystem which are quite site specific, some of which need to be modified by a site even when the primary site of the root is not available. Accounting files dominate the list. To accomodate such files, while preserving the primary site replicated root environment, the system uses a per-machine subtree and some special symbolic links, both described below.

Each site is given a small subtree in the global file system referred to as that site's "local file system". Files like the standard Unix utmp and wtmp files, daemon log files, spool subdirectories, a dev directory and the tmp subdirectory are contained in the local file system.

While all these files and directories have globally unique names, some application programs and users may expect them to have the historical names in the root (e.g. utmp is usually /etc/utmp). While a violation of transparency, programs or users can issue one name and have it mapped to a different name, depending on the machine it is issued from. For example, /etc/utmp issued on bilbo will give /bilbo/utmp while on frodo it gives /frodo/utmp. To accomplish this mapping, certain file names in the replicated root are symbolic links of the form *<LOCAL>/filename* (eg. <LOCAL>/utmp). In addition, each process inherits a translation for <LOCAL> (on bilbo it would translate to /bilbo). System calls *setlocal* and *getlocal* manipulate and interrogate the translation value of <LOCAL> (see Appendix A).

The result of this mechanism is binary and source compatibility on the one hand while still maintaining that all files do have a globally unique name and are thus accessible anywhere on the net.

Note that it is not necessary for a site in a LOCUS network to have local storage media to make use of this facility, since the node's <LOCAL> variable can be set at boot time to any appropriate point in the name hierarchy, and thus to storage anywhere in the network.

3.10.3   Accessing Remote Devices

In a distributed operating system such as LOCUS, it is desirable that devices, like other resources, be accessible remotely in a transparent manner. In LOCUS, that is the general approach. Device names appear in the single, global naming hierarchy. That is, each device has a globally unique path name, just as other named resources do.[1]

The implementation of transparent remote devices has two important parts. First is the naming and locating part. That is similar to any other type of entry in the catalog system. Pathname search is done until the inode for the device is found. An internal open is done, and a copy of the inode is placed in memory at the storage site (the site where the device is located) as well as at the using site (where the request was made).

The second part of remote device operation is the support for the actual operations that are needed. We distinguish three types of devices: *buffered block, buffered character,* and *unbuffered.* A buffered block device is one for which the system is responsible for managing reading and writing of the device in standard sized blocks, and the actual device operation is asynchronous from the caller. Unix block devices, including a number of direct memory access (dma) peripherals, fit this category. Support for transparent buffered devices is present in LOCUS in the current implementation. The necessary mechanism is little different from that needed for file support. Remote device access is of course rather valuable. For example, the dump and archive software on LOCUS need not be any different from such software for a single-machine Unix system. Compare this situation of "no additional work needed" with the dumping strategies used in less integrated networks. Transparent remote and local block device support is an important part of the LOCUS architecture.

Terminals are the best example of buffered character devices. In the case of a terminal local to the program accessing it, the kernel queues both incoming and outgoing characters, with some processing (e.g., echoing) done by the terminal driver portion of the kernel. Remote terminals are not substantially different. Data from the terminal is queued only until a remote read message arrives. Then the data is sent to the requesting site and process as a response to the outstanding read. Writes from the remote process are sent to the site of the device for queueing to the device. The terminal driver at the site to which the terminal is physically connected is always responsible for character processing.

There are three major differences between handling remote buffered block and character devices. First, of course, is that the number of bytes transferred is variable in the character case. Second, remote read requests in the character case must be handled specially, because it may take an arbitrary time to complete, waiting for user input. Third, it is necessary to provide a means for programs to communicate with remote terminal drivers to indicate the mode in which the terminal is to run. Transparent remote

---

[1] Each site will usually have its own /dev directory which is also globally named. A discussion of this was given in the previous section.

and local character devices are included in the LOCUS architecture.

The third class of device is *unbuffered*. Data is transferred directly from the process's data image to the device. Large data reads or writes can be done in one I/O, so tape drives, for example, are often treated as unbuffered devices. While it is certainly possible to construct a means of accessing remote unbuffered devices, it would require setting up a large buffer space at the device home site and sending across the data one block at a time. One reason for this is that typical local area network hardware cannot handle large messages. By having to buffer at the device site, however, one loses much of the advantage of dealing with an unbuffered device. Instead, if at all possible, one would like in this case to move the process to the data instead of the data to the process. Consequently, LOCUS does not support remote unbuffered device access.

3.10.4   Node failures

Whenever a node is lost from an operational LOCUS network, cleanup work is necessary. If a CSS for a given filegroup is lost, another site must take over this role and must gather from all the remaining storage sites of the filegroup the status of all open files in that filegroup. In addition, all open inodes involving the lost sites must be cleaned up at all remaining sites. This action is the reason why all storage sites keep per-file state information indicating which other sites have a given file open. Certain data pages must be discarded, and those processes involved in modification of a remote file which is no longer available must be aborted. Processes reading a remote file whose storage site has been lost may continue if another storage site for that file remains available. There are a number of other actions which are also necessary. Chapter 5 has more information on these issues.

3.11   Summary

The LOCUS file system, with its transparent name management, is the heart of the distributed system mechanisms. This architectural choice was made both because file system functions such as name management are needed by so many other parts of a distributed system, and because data access behavior so often dominates overall system performance. Not layering such a function over other facilities reduces overhead.

4 Remote Tasking

LOCUS permits one to execute programs at any site in the network, subject to permission control, in a manner just as easy as executing the program locally. In fact, one can dynamically, even just before process invocation, select the execution site. It is also possible to request that an already running process move (migrate) from one site to another of the same cpu type. The mechanism is entirely transparent, so that existing software can be executed either locally or remotely, with no change to that software. No load module relinking or any other action is required. This transparency makes remote execution of a program, as well as the construction and execution of distributed programs, or dynamic loadleveling, exceedingly straightforward.

To achieve transparency, several issues must be addressed. First a user interface must be designed. It must be easy to use, and it must be compatible with standard Unix. A high degree of flexibility is also required.

Second, a method is needed to uniquely specify a process. This is achieved through unique process names. Uniqueness is assured by partitioning the name space between different sites on the network.

Also, protocols must be designed to copy or move processes across the network. These protocols must not only be efficient, but they must also maintain compatibility with single site Unix.

Finally, a method is needed to be able to keep track of which processes exist and where they exist. Knowing which processes exist is needed so that uniqueness of process names is maintained. The location of the processes is needed for interprocess communication.

4.1 User View

The major process control functions have been extended from Unix in an upward compatible way. Unix contains a *fork* call, which creates a new process running the same program with the same data as the caller. The Unix *exec* call replaces the code and data of a running process with a new program and data image. Most often, in typical Unix applications, a *fork* call is quickly followed by an *exec* call. In LOCUS, both of these calls are available. *Fork* can cause a new process to be created locally or remotely.

Exec has been extended to allow a process to migrate to another site as it replaces its image. A third call, *run*, has been added. It is intended to achieve the effect of a combination of *fork* and *exec* from a logical point of view. *Run* creates a new process and invokes a new program in it immediately. *Run* can be used to initiate execution locally or remotely, just as with *exec*. Additionally, a fourth call, *migrate*, has been added to permit a process to change its site of execution while in the midst of execution. Clearly, remote *fork* and *migrate* can be done only between matching cpu types, since the process retains substantial internal state information. By contrast, the cpu types of the source and destination sites of either an *exec* or a *run* may differ.

In all of these cases, the decision about where the new process is to execute is specified by information associated with the calling process that can be set dynamically by a *setxsites* call. This function sets up a list of sites which *fork*, *exec*, *run*, and *migrate* use to select the execution site. In this way, a running program can set where its subprocesses will execute. LOCUS provides to the user several simple programs which first set the execution list according to some criteria (e.g., a user-specified site or the fastest available site) and then *exec* the user-specified program with the user's arguments.

Use of an additional system call to set execution site information was chosen, rather than adding arguments to the existing calls, for two reasons. First, by not changing existing system call interfaces, software written with the old system calls continues to work, and in fact may have its execution site externally controlled. This aspect is especially valuable when source code is not available. Also, separating such a facility into a separate call, rather than having it be part of several system calls, was considered simpler to use.

In some cases it may be desirable to migrate a process after it has begun execution. It should even be possible to do this to a program which knows nothing of the *migrate* system call. This can be accomplished by sending a special signal, *SIGMIGRATE*, to the process. Since it is necessary for this signal to identify the site to which the process should move, an extended form of Unix's *kill* system call must be provided. This call, *kill3*, takes an additional argument which specifies the new site. An advantage of using Unix's existing signaling mechanism is that it is possible to move a set of related processes by sending *SIGMIGRATE* to a process group or to all processes created by the same user. Once a process receives a *SIGMIGRATE*, the default action is for the process to migrate itself to the specified site, as if it had executed a *migrate* system call. It is also possible for the process to ignore the signal or for it to catch the signal and perform some special action (e.g., changing its local directory before migrating).

Overall, these facilities make distributed processing mechanisms quite easy for applications to use. In the sections below, we discuss the issues involved in remote process execution and the resulting implementation.

4.2 Process Naming

To ensure that processes can be addressed unambiguously in cross-network references, and that multiple processes are not created with the same process identifier (PID), one has to extend the local process name by some unique identifier to distinguish between different sites. LOCUS process naming allows each site of the network to autonomously assign names to the processes which originate at that site. Obviously, a site address could be used for a unique site identifier (SID). Thus, under a localized process naming scheme, network-wide process names could be made up by combining a Unix-like local PID with an SID to form a Network PID (see Figure 4-1). Since processes can migrate, the content of the name does not indicate the current site of execution. The SID only identifies the site on which the process originated, so no compromise in transparency has been made.

network process identifier

site identifier	*local* process identifier

Figure 4-1: Contents of a Network Process Name

In Unix, processes are placed in process groups whose names (PGRPs) usually match the PID of the "leader" of the group. Since this arrangement is also used in LOCUS, PGRPs also contain an SID which specifies the site on which the group originated; thus process group names are also assured to be unique.

4.3   Network Processes

The four types of remote process system calls can be categorized in two different ways. *Fork* and *migrate* both copy all of the information about the process. This information includes the ''proc'' and ''user'' structures, user data, and user stack[1]. Since the new process on the destination site will continue executing the same program using the same data, *fork* and *migrate* can only be used between sites with similar hardware architectures.

The only process data that *exec* and *run* need to copy is the process and user structures; however, it is also necessary for them to transmit the command line arguments and process environment. These calls will both begin execution of a new program, so it is possible for either of these calls to be used between any two sites, regardless of hardware differences between them.

On the other hand, we can group these functions according to the processes which are created. *Fork* and *run* create new processes on the destination site while allowing the old process to continue executing on the source site. The new process will be a child of the old process. *Exec* and *migrate* destroy the process on the source site, replacing it with the new process on the destination site. Figure 4-2 tabulates the categorization of these functions.

	old image	new image
move old process	*migrate*	*exec*
create new child	*fork*	*run*

Figure 4-2: Remote Process System Calls

---

[1] In general, it is not necessary to copy the executable code. See the ''Remote Process Protocol Design'', section 4.3.2.1.

4.3.1 Modification of Process Data Structures

Three major steps are necessary to handle remote forks. First, each process needs to have a unique ID which is valid throughout the entire system, i.e. the network. As explained above, the easiest way to create such an ID is by combining the Unix process number with a unique site identification code. In order to ensure complete transparency, LOCUS returns a complete Network PID whenever Unix applications look at PIDs.

A second modification was required to allow a parent process to keep track of its children in a network environment. In LOCUS a parent may have children existing at a collection of different sites. One has to make sure that communications from the parent to its offspring will reach all processes involved. This is achieved by giving each parent a "remote children list," which specifies the location of each remote child.

Finally, it is often necessary to send a message to a specific process. For example, a child process must be able to notify its parent upon exiting. Signals must also be able to be directed to any single process or group of processes. The originating site must, therefore, retain some state information regarding processes which are forked or executed remotely (see "Process Tracking", section 4.5).

4.3.2 Remote Process Implementation

In this section, we present the implementation mechanisms needed to support the distributed process functionality which has been outlined. First, we look at the intersite protocol, and then examine matters from the source and destinations sites' points of view.

4.3.2.1 Remote Process Protocol Design

The overall strategy for the transmission of the code image of the parent process is based on a *pulling* protocol. This is to say that once the parent process has issued a request for a fork at some remote site, that site will take control and be responsible for paging the image of the parent process across the network. In particular, this means that the parent process is suspended after a "Fork Process Request" (FPR) message has been positively acknowledged by the site named as the destination site. The destination site will begin to send request messages to the source site in order to have the parent's process image or environment paged over the network. Paging of the process image is thus strictly by demand and in standard sized blocks.

The FPR message is a generic message which does not require a specific process to receive it. It includes the parts of the parent's 'proc' and 'user' structures that will be needed by the child, along with open file information. This is the only exception to the *pulling* protocol.

At the parent site, requests for portions of the process image are received by the network interrupt driver. The interrupt driver is able to determine what process image is being paged and thus can awaken the parent process. By examining the type of the child's request the parent can then determine what data to send to the child site. The following requests may be issued by the child site:

SPDTA —   page the user data and stack (*fork* and *migrate*),
SENV —   page the command line and environment (*exec* and *run*),
FRKDNE —   the network process request is complete (all request types).

The details of the protocol will be described in the following sections. It is also summarized in Figure 4-3.

Note that none of the message types cover the case of paging executable code. Since LOCUS handles shared code by giving each of the processes involved a descriptor for the shared text segment, it follows that the system will exercise particular discretion at the child site as to how to obtain a copy of the shared text. If the text is pure (unwritable), it will be obtained by opening the file using the protocols of Chapter 3. If the text is impure, it will be treated as part of the user data and will be read using the SPDTA messages.

The major advantage of the *pulling* nature of the above protocol is that no buffering of process data is required at the child site. A request for another page of the parent's process image will be issued only when the child site is ready to receive it. Considering that buffer space is often a limited resource, the advantages of this strategy should be clear.

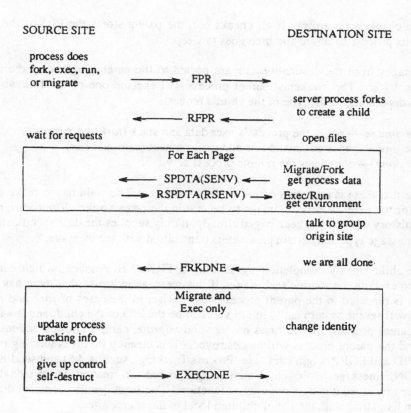

SOURCE SITE   DESTINATION SITE

process does
fork, exec, run,
or migrate   ——————→ FPR ——————→
                                                    server process forks
                                                    to create a child
                        ←—————— RFPR ←——————
wait for requests   open files

| For Each Page |
| Migrate/Fork get process data |

←—————— SPDTA(SENV) ←——————   Migrate/Fork
                                  get process data
——————→ RSPDTA(RSENV) ——————→ Exec/Run
                                  get environment
                                                    talk to group
                                                    origin site

                                                    we are all done
                        ←—————— FRKDNE ←——————

                        Migrate and
                        Exec only
update process   change identity
tracking info

give up control
self-destruct   ——————→ EXECDNE ——————→

Figure 4-3: Remote Process Creation

4.3.2.2 Remote Processes at the Source Site

A *fork*, *exec*, *run*, or *migrate* across the network is initiated by a call to the corresponding system routine. This routine picks a site using the execution site list (see "Site Selection", section 4.3.3). The chosen site parameter is checked for its validity. If the chosen site is local, a call is made to the local version of the routine (except for *migrate*, which does nothing in the local case). Invalid and null sites return an error code to the user program. Parameter values which indicate a remote site activate the routine *net_proc*.

Net_proc is the only routine actively executed by the parent process during a remote fork. It starts by sending a FPR message to the destination site which includes a flag indicating what type of remote call (*fork*, *exec*, *run*, or *migrate*) is taking place. This message also includes the "proc" and "user" structures. When the response comes in, it is first checked for errors. If all checks out, the parent stores the PID of the remote child in its process structure and then goes to sleep.

Messages from the destination site are posted to the parent process by the network interrupt driver. The awakened parent process will execute one of the following three routines depending on the type of the child's request:

> *page_image* — pages the process's user data and stack (*fork* and *migrate*),
> *page_env* — pages command line and environment (*exec* and *run*),
> *fork_done* — completes the remote process service.

Note that there is no error control on the source site. The child has to make sure that it asks for the parent's process image to be sent in the proper order. The parent does not store a history of what has been paged already; it only supplies the data specifically asked for by message type and certain parameters transmitted with the message.

The child signals completion by sending a FRKDNE message, which causes the parent to execute the routine *fork_done*. If this message indicates that there has been an error, it is reported to the parent process. Otherwise, in the cases of *fork* and *run*, this routine will set the system call's return value to be the PID of the child; and it will return to the parent process. In the cases of *exec* and *migrate*, certain cleanup actions will be done and the parent process will be destroyed. This cleanup involves sending messages to the PID and PGRP origin sites (see 'Process Tracking', section 4.5) and sending a final EXECDNE message to the child containing updated information about signals which have been received during the *net_proc* function. This message also contains the remote children list, along with the list of children local to the source site.

4.3.2.3 Remote Processes at the Destination Site

At the remote site the FPR message sent by *net_proc* is received by a server process. Upon receipt of this message, the server process forks a child process which will, for the time being, execute in kernel mode and be responsible for obtaining the necessary data from the parent process.

First, the child process updates its 'user' and 'proc' structures, opens the files the parent is using, and stores the obtained kernel stack information. When the child opens the parent's files, however, this is a special type of open. As a child on the same site as its parent would bypass access protection checks and obtain a reference to the same file offset structure, so must this remote child. Thus, the file offset token mechanism described in chapter 3 is used to set up another copy of the parent's file offset structure on this site for the child. If the child is being created on a site which already has a copy of the shared file offset structure, the token manager site will know this and the child will be told to use it. All this makes the child process appear to be a true child of the parent process.

At this stage the remote child needs to check what kind of remote process request this is (*fork*, *exec*, etc.) in order to determine which other data has to be obtained from the parent. If a *fork* or *migrate* call is in progress, the routine *rec_image* is invoked to copy the user area of the parent process (the user area consists of the user data and the user stack). By repeatedly sending SPDTA messages, *rec_image* copies the user area in standard sized blocks and stores it in the virtual memory space allocated prior to the call to *rec_image*. *Rec_image* is in sole control of this copying process. For this reason it must forward to the source site all parameters which uniquely identify the pages currently requested. Also, upon receipt of a response, *rec_image* must check that the message does contain the requested pages.

In the *fork* and *migrate* cases, it is not necessary to read the program text. By checking other data already obtained, the child process can determine the load module of the parent and its type (pure or impure text). If the load module being executed by the parent is pure, existing LOCUS system routines allow for obtaining a copy. If the load module is impure it is part of the user area and will be automatically paged from the parent when a copy of the user area is requested.

On the other hand, *exec* and *run* do not need to copy any part of the parent's user area. They will get the text and data from the text file. They do, however, need to get the command arguments and environment. These are paged over using SENV messages in a manner very similar to the paging scheme used for SPDTA.

When the necessary data from the parent process has been transferred, the child notifies the parent with a FRKDNE message that the network process request is complete. Some special handling is done, however, for the *exec* and *migrate* cases. Until this point, the process on the destination site has appeared to be a child of the process on the source site. The "child" will now change its identity to make it "turn into" the parent. This requires changing the PID, the parent PID, and the PGRP. Also, after sending the FRKDNE message, the new process must wait for the "parent" to send a EXECDNE message containing signals that were delivered during the remote process transfer.

At this point all that remains is for the child to "return" to user code. Since the child really began as a child of a server process, it cannot just issue a return instruction. Instead some care must be taken to clean up the stack in order to get back to running the user code.

4.3.3 Site Selection

The decision regarding the site at which a process is to run is influenced by several factors. First, the user may wish to exercise control, either advisory or absolute, over the site, or set of sites, from which execution choice can be made. Second, there are physical constraints on where execution is possible. Finally, additional constraints may be added to assist with administrative control. In particular, certain users may only be given permission to execute programs on certain sites.

The user can control the site where his processes are executed in several ways. First, the default is for execution to take place locally, i.e., at the site where the creating process is already running. Second, the user may request that an already running process move by sending a *SIGMIGRATE* signal to the process. Finally, associated with each process is an environment, which includes such items as the user's working directory, search list for hidden directories, and, of interest here, execution site list. The site list can be specified by the system call *setxsites*. This call allows the specification of a specific site or a list of sites to be tried in order. The environment is inherited by children processes, so that a remote fork to site I, for example, will automatically have its environment set so that subsequent forks will tend to take place locally at site I. Shell commands are also available to set the environment.

After load module selection is made (possibly through a hidden directory), the module type is checked to determine on which site type it can run. The system then tries to execute the given load module at the specified site, in the order they are given in the site list. Reasons for failure to execute at a given site include:

    a. site not available,
    b. local autonomy control does not permit execution,
    c. site type not compatible with load module selected,
    d. site type not compatible with current load module (in the case of fork).

Permission for a user to execute on a particular site is granted by the *setxperm* system call. The *getxperm* system call allows application programs to see which sites may be used. *setxperm*, which is restricted to the super user, is called by the *login* program. The resulting xperm list is inherited by children and may only be modified by another call to setxperm.

4.4 Swapping and Paging

LOCUS supports both swapping and paging. For those machines which can take and recover from page faults, paging is usually the desired choice. For machines which cannot (and there are many in this class), swapping must be used. Some machines have the capability of recovering properly from page faults on program text, but cannot recover from faults for program data. While LOCUS does not currently contain special support for those machines, a mixed strategy can be easily provided for that case.

LOCUS can be configured with three versions of the swapping/paging code: paging, bulk swapping, and page swapping. In the paging case, pages of processes are brought into memory on a demand basis and placed in any free page frames available. If the hardware can support virtual memory larger than real memory, then LOCUS also allows the users to take advantage of the illusion of virtual memory. The page replacement algorithms are isolated and can easily be tailored to take advantage of any least recently used or other page replacement hardware support provided. If no hardware support is available (as is the case on the DEC VAX), a general replacement algorithm is provided.

For machines which cannot support page faults, the entire process must be brought into memory before being run. In the bulk swapping configuration, the various pieces of a process (code, data, stack, user structure) must each be stored in contiguous portions of real memory. A minimum number of I/O operations are performed to swap a process in or out. When no contiguous space is available to load a process, memory compaction (with its associated copying of memory) may be used to eliminate fragmentation, or processes can be swapped out to make room. In the bulk swapping configuration, memory reorganization (with its associated copying of a process image) is also required when process memory sizes change, for example during the *sbrk* function or when growing the user stack.

The system can also be configured for page swapping. In this mode, the system takes advantage of the page-oriented relocation hardware available on some machines even though those machines cannot recover from page faults. Programs are loaded into whatever page frames are available, and those pages are then mapped to give the illusion of a contiguous process memory space. As with bulk swapping, however, the entire process must be resident because of the hardware restrictions. If memory mapped I/O hardware is available on the machine, then the reading of the process can be performed again in a minimum number of I/O operations. Otherwise, the process pages must be individually read in, or copied to the destination frames. Memory mapped I/O is also required to allow raw I/O directly to user space. Page swapping has the advantages of better memory utilization and better performance. No memory compactions are required and certain operations, such as *sbrk* or user stack growth no longer require the memory copying which occurs in standard swapping systems. Memory copying only occurs during the *fork* and *run* system calls, as required by the semantics of that function.

During an *exec*, if the text file is not stored at the execution site, it would be possible, on a paging system, to demand page across the network. LOCUS does not currently support this scheme. Instead the entire file is read and saved on the swap device before execution begins.

4.5 Process Tracking

As processes move around the network, various sites and other processes need to know where the migrating processes are. In these sections, we lay out how this record keeping is done and how it is used, including behavior in the face of failures.

4.5.1 Sending a Message to a Specified Process

There is a variety of circumstances under which interprocess communication (IPC) is desirable. Often the sending process knows only the PID of the destination process. In the local case, this condition is handled by a simple search of the process table. A hashing algorithm is employed to make this search more efficient.

The remote equivalent of a search through the process table would be to broadcast the message to all other sites and to have each site search its own table. Besides being inefficient, such a broadcast would lead to problems if the destination process is migrating message transmission. The message may be received by the process on both sites or on neither site.

The solution used by LOCUS is to assign a synchronization site for each process. The network PID employed earlier to assure unique network names for processes includes a site identifier (SID) which specifies the site on which the process was created. This origin site (OSITE) is then used as the synchronization site for the process. If the real origin site, as specified by the SID, is not currently on the network, then a surrogate origin site is used. All sites on the network agree in advance which one will act as surrogate.

The basic mechanism for sending a message to a process is then straightforward. First the process is checked for locally, using the hashing mentioned above. If it is not found, a message is sent to the origin site (or surrogate site). If the process is there, the message is delivered to the process and any return value for the message is returned to the sender. If the process is not at the OSITE, a message is sent back indicating the site at which the process will be found. Finally the message is sent to the specified site.

Several factors necessitate an enhanced mechanism. First, between the time that the OSITE sends the response specifying the retry site and the time that the message is resent to that site, the process may have migrated away. Thus, if a retry message fails to find the process, it is necessary to go back and ask the OSITE for the new location of the process.

Second, the network configuration might change (see chapter 5, "Dynamic Reconfiguration of LOCUS") while trying to find a process. In particular, the sender may be trying to send to a surrogate origin site just as the real origin site comes back onto the network. In this case the surrogate site will send back an error code indicating that it is no longer responsible for the specified process. The sender will need to recalculate the OSITE from the process's SID and start over.

A final problem also occurs during network reconfiguration. Even after sending to the real origin site (which has just returned to the network), the origin site may not have had a chance to collect all of the data relating to the locations of its remote processes. In this case a return code is sent back indicating that the sender should wait and try again shortly.

4.5.2 Process Group Tracking

Unix provides for process groups. These are groups of associated processes which share a common name, the PGRP. The PGRP is usually the PID of the process considered to be the "group leader." In order to make sure that PGRPs are unique, it is necessary to avoid creating a process with a PID that matches any existing PGRPs. Otherwise, if that process were to become a group leader, it would unknowingly join the previously extant PGRP.

In Unix it is possible to send a signal to all of the processes in a given group. In the local case this is handled by a search of the entire process table. As with signals to a single process, the remote equivalent would be to broadcast the signal to all sites in order to find all of the members of the group. This is undesirable for the same reasons given above. Thus it is necessary to track process groups in order to achieve unique group names and in order to properly signal the members of a remote process group.

On LOCUS, since PIDs contain a site identifier, so do PGRPs. Thus it is possible to track the processes in the group by using the group origin site (GOSITE) as the synchronization site. The same site which serves as surrogate OSITE also serves as surrogate GOSITE.

Each site will have a list of remote processes that originated there, and for each process it will have the site at which the process will be found. Each site also has a list of PGRPs which originated there, and for each PGRP it has a list of sites at which group members will be found. In order to send a message to all of the members of a group, it is necessary to send to each site in the GOSITE's list.

The same problem mentioned above that occurs if one were to try to find a process by broadcasting to all sites will occur here in sending to a process group. If a group member is migrating while the message is being sent, the process may receive the message twice or not at all. To avoid this, the GOSITE will forbid any member of the group to migrate while a message is being sent to the group.

The method for sending a message to a group is therefore as follows. If the sender is at the GOSITE, lock out all migrates for this group, check for local members of the group, send the message to each other site at which a group member exists, and finally unlock migrates. If the sender is not at the GOSITE, the message is sent to the GOSITE, which proceeds to do the work described above. As in the normal process tracking case, the sender must be prepared to recalculate the GOSITE and resend the message in case the network is being reconfigured.

4.5.3 Updating the Process Tracking Data Base

Tracking processes and process groups requires maintaining a list of remote processes (or PGRPs) along with the site(s) on which they reside. These lists will change whenever a process changes sites (from a *fork*, *exec*, *run*, *migrate*, or *SIGMIGRATE*) or when a remote process exits. The lists must also be updated after a network reconfiguration.

4.5.3.1 Updating During Processes Migration

From the destination site of a network process, a message is sent to the GOSITE requesting permission to migrate. This message is sent just before the FRKDNE message is sent to the source site. In addition to requesting permission, it also notifies the GOSITE that there is at least one member of the process group at this site.

If the network process function is *exec* or *migrate*, then after the FRKDNE arrives at the source site, several process tracking messages are sent:

PSORIG to the process's origin site,
PSORIG to the process's group origin site,
PSPAR to the parent's site.

The message to the OSITE is not sent if the OSITE is the same as the destination site (the data base will be updated by the network process code on that site). The message to the GOSITE is sent only if there are no more process group members on the source site. The message to the parent is sent so that the parent can maintain its remote children list. This list is used when the parent issues a *wait* system call and when it exits (see section 4.5.3.3).

4.5.3.2 Updating During Network Reconfiguration

When the network is reconfigured, the process tracking data can be out of date for several reasons. When site X returns to the network, there may be processes on other sites which originated at site X before it went down. The situation is even worse if two partitions, previously separated by, say, a broken network connection, come together onto a single network.

The simplest approach to recovering the process tracking data would be for every site to tell every other site about any remote processes (if any) which it has that originated on the other site. This approach, however, would result in heavy loading of the network resources. Performance could be improved by having each site notify only the OSITEs and GOSITEs of all of the processes running on that site. The problem would then be that each site would not know when it had finished receiving all of its data. Failure to receive information from another site could mean that it has no processes which originated here, or it could just be the result of a slow network connection.

LOCUS employs the second method described above, with a small amount of extra work so that each site will know exactly which sites will be sending it data. During the network reconfiguration protocol, one site acts as the *active* site. Each site sends a message (PMOUNT) to the active site indicating which file systems are mounted locally. The active site collects all of this information and sends the complete mount table to each site using a NEWTOP message. Process tracking takes advantage of this protocol by having each site include in its PMOUNT message a list of sites to which it plans to send process tracking data. The active site correlates this data, and when it sends the NEWTOP message to each site, it includes the list of sites which will be sending messages to that site.

As mentioned above, if a message comes to a site asking about a process which originated there before the site has collected all of its data, the response will indicate that the sender should try again later. This response will be sent if the message was received in between a point early in reconfiguration procedure after which the process tracking data may be incomplete and the point at which the site has received data from all sites from which it is expecting data. Furthermore, to make sure that the process tracking data that is sent is always complete, migrates are held up during this time.

4.5.3.3   Updating During Processes Termination

When a process terminates it is necessary to close all files it had open, to release its memory space, to notify its parent, and to make certain status information (e.g., exit status and cpu time) available for the parent to look at. All of the process's children must also be notified that their parent has died.

In the case of a process with a local parent the system has a straightforward task at hand. The cleaning-up is easy to do, and the process table entry of the terminating process can simply be overlaid with the exit status. Notifying local children is also simple, requiring a search of the process table to find all processes with the specified parent. The *exit* system call performs these functions.

If *exit* finds that the parent is already waiting for a child, the system will wake him up. When the parent process runs again it will find the child, examine the exit status, and then release the process table entry which once pointed to the deceased child. On the other hand, if the parent is not waiting, the system relies on the parent to eventually execute a *wait* system call in order to find out about the fate of its children.

Note that this mechanism applies also to such cases where the parent has died without waiting for all of its children. Here the children will be inherited by the local *init* process which, so to speak, waits for every process in the system and thus can clean up deceased orphans.

In the network environment the parent of a terminating child may be running at a remote site. If this is the case, a message is sent to the parent. This message is of the same type as that used to notify the parent of a migrate (PSPAR), except that instead of specifying a new site, a code is sent indicating that the process is exiting. (If the parent site is down, a previous network reconfiguration will have changed the process to be a child of the local *init* process.)

When a parent issues a *wait* system call, first it will look for any local children that have died. If it has none, it will look for an entry in its remote children list indicating that a remote child has died. If so, it will send a message (WAIT) to that site to find out the exit status. Since the dead child cannot migrate, the parent's list is guaranteed to have the correct site.

During a parent's *exit* call, all of the parent's children must be notified that their parent has died. Each of the children will then be inherited by the local *init* process. This notification is done by searching through the process table to find all local children. Then for each remote site specified in the remote children list, a message (ABNDN) is sent to that site requesting that all children on that site be abandoned. The response to this message indicates the PIDs of the abandoned children that have been found. These children are removed from the list, and the message is resent until there are no more children.

4.6 Signals

Signals are software interrupts that can be posted to processes. They can be generated in three different ways: (1) by the system as the result of a hardware condition (e.g., floating point overflow or invalid memory address), (2) by another process using the *kill* or *kill3* system calls, and (3) by the terminal driver when certain keys are typed. In the first case, the signal is always delivered to the current process. In the second case, the process tracking and process group tracking methods described above are used in a very straightforward manner.

In the case of signals generated by terminal interrupts, however, a problem arises. The interrupt handler cannot be made to wait for network resources to become available, so it cannot send messages to other sites. To avoid this problem a special kernel process, the *signet daemon*, is used to send these messages. The interrupt driver simply posts the information describing the signal to the *daemon*'s queue and wakes up the *daemon*. All of the work of sending messages to the GOSITE is handled through the *daemon*.

A special optimization is used for the local case. If the GOSITE is local and if the process group tracking data base indicates that there are no remote processes, the signal is posted to the local process group members by the interrupt driver. This avoids the overhead of waking up the *daemon* and ensures that the signals are delivered as fast as possible.

4.7 Summary

Much of the work involved in support of transparent tasking in LOCUS results from the failure modes and race conditions inherent in the distributed environment. However, by providing these facilities in a transparent manner, users are accorded a convenient tool without being burdened with the underlying complexities.

5 Dynamic Reconfiguration of LOCUS

The transparency goal in LOCUS applies not only to the static configuration of the network, but to the configuration changes themselves. The system strives to insulate the users from reconfigurations, providing continuing operation with only negligible delay. Just as in normal operation, requiring user programs to deal with reconfiguration would shift the network costs from the single operating system to the multiple applications programs.

This chapter discusses the concept of transparency as it relates to a dynamic network environment, gives several principles that the operating system should follow to provide it, and presents the reconfiguration protocols used in LOCUS. The protocols make use of a high-level synchronization strategy to avoid the message overhead of conventional two-phased commits and are largely independent of the specific details of LOCUS.

The normal operation protocols of LOCUS assume that the underlying network is fully connected. If site A can communicate with site B, and site B with site C, then site A is assumed able to communicate with site C. In practice, this communication may be done by routing messages from A to C through B, and the present implementation of LOCUS is able to forward packets in this manner. The assumption of transitivity of communication significantly simplifies the protocols used in LOCUS.

The low-level protocols enforce that network transitivity. Network information is kept internally in both a status table and a collection of virtual circuits.[1] The two structures are, to some extent, independent. Membership in the partition does not guarantee the existence of a virtual circuit, nor does an open virtual circuit guarantee membership in the partition. Failure of a virtual circuit, either on or after open, does, however, remove a node from a partition. Likewise, removal from a partition closes all relevant virtual circuits. All changes in partitions invoke the protocols discussed later in this chapter.

---

[1] The virtual circuits deliver messages from *site* A to *site* B (the virtual circuits connect sites, not processes) in the order they are sent.

5.1 Requirements for the Reconfiguration Protocols

The first constraint on the reconfiguration protocol is that it maintain consistency with respect to the internal system protocols. All solutions satisfying this constraint could be termed correct. Correctness, however, is not enough. In addition to maintaining system integrity, the solution must insulate the user from the underlying system changes. The solution should not affect program development, and it should be efficient enough that any delays it imposes are negligible.

Optimally, the reconfiguration algorithms should not affect the user in any manner whatsoever. A user accessing resources on machine A from machine B should not be affected by any activity involving machine C. This intuitive idea can be expressed in several principles:

a. User activity should be allowed to continue without adverse affect, provided no resources are lost.

b. Any delay imposed by the system on user activity during reconfiguration should be negligible.

c. The user should be shielded from any transient effects of the network configuration.

d. Any activity initiated after the reconfiguration should reflect the state of the system after the reconfiguration.

e. Specialized users should be able to detect reconfigurations if necessary.

f. No user should be penalized for increased availability of resources.[1]

All these principles are fairly intuitive. They merely extend the concept of network transparency to a dynamic network and express a desire for efficiency. They do, however, tightly constrain the eventual algorithms. For example, those operations with high delay potentials must be partitioned in such a way that the tasks relevant to a specific user request can be run quickly, efficiently, and immediately. The LOCUS architecture is oriented toward support of these principles, and generally succeeds very well.

---

[1] This last point may cause violations of synchronization policies, as discussed below.

The principles have far-reaching implications in areas such as file access and synchronization. Suppose, for example, a process were reading from a file replicated twice in its partition. If it were to lose contact with the copy it was reading, the system should substitute the other copy (assuming, of course, that it is still available).

5.2 Protocol Structure

As noted before, the underlying LOCUS protocols assume a fully connected network. To ensure correct operation, the reconfiguration strategy tries to guarantee this property. If, for instance, a momentary break occurs between two sites, all other sites in the partition must be notified of the break. A simple scan of available nodes is insufficient.

The present strategy splits the reconfiguration into two protocols: the *partition* protocol, which is run to find fully connected subnetworks when a failure has occurred; and the *merge* protocol, which is run to merge several such subnetworks into a fuller partition. This organization was selected to allow the possibility of running just the partition protocol when a failure occurred or just the merge protocol when a site wanted to join the network. Currently both protocols are run if any reconfiguration is needed. The partition protocol affects only those sites previously thought to be up. If necessary, it divides a partition into two subpartitions, each of which is guaranteed to be fully connected and disjoint from the other. It detects all site and communications failures and cleans up all affected multisite data structures, so that the merge protocol can ignore such matters. The merge protocol polls the set of available sites, and merges several disjoint subpartitions into one.

After the new partition is established, the reconciliation procedure corrects any inconsistencies brought about either by the reconfiguration code itself, or by activity while the network was not connected. Reconciliation is concerned mainly with file consistency. It detects modifications and schedules update propagation.

All reconfiguration protocols are controlled by a high-priority kernel process. The partition and merge protocols are run directly by that process, while the reconciliation procedure runs as a privileged application program.

5.3 The Partition Protocol

Communication in a fully connected network is an equivalence relation. Thus the partitions we speak about are partitions of the set of nodes of the network, in the strict, mathematical sense. In normal operation, the site tables reflect the equivalence classes: all members of a partition agree on the status of the general network. When a communication break occurs, for whatever reason, these tables become unsynchronized. The partition code must reestablish the logical partitioning that the operating system assumes, and synchronize the site tables of its member sites to reflect the new environment.

In general, a communication failure between any two sites does not imply a failure of either site. Failures caused by transmission noise or unforeseen delays cannot be detected directly by foreign sites, and will often be detected in only one of the sites involved. In such situations, the partition algorithm should find maximum partitions: a single communications failure should not result in the network breaking into three or more parts.[1] LOCUS implements a solution based on iterative intersection.

A few terms are helpful for the following discussion. The *partition set*, P_α, is the set of sites believed up by site α. The *new partition set*, NP_α, is the set of sites known by α to have joined the new partition.

Consider a partition P after some set of failures has occurred. To form a new partition, the sites must reach a consensus on the state of the network. The criterion for consensus may be stated in set notation as: for every $\alpha,\beta \in P$, $P_\alpha = P_\beta$. This state can be reached from any initial condition by taking successive intersections of the partition sets of a group of sites.

When a site α runs the partition algorithm, it polls the sites in P_α and incrementally forms a new partition set NP_α. Initially NP_α just has α in it. As α polls β, β indicates it's partition set P_β. If P_β includes all the sites in NP_α, β can be added to the sites in NP_α. However, now α cannot add any sites to NP_α that were not in P_β so P_α (α's polling set) is modified to be $P_\alpha \cap P_\beta$. The sites which are to be polled and potentially included in

---

[1] Breaking a virtual circuit between two sites aborts any ongoing activity between those two sites. Partition fragmentation must be minimized to minimize the loss of work.

NP_α are those sites in P_α which are not already in NP_α. As an example, consider α as 1 and P_1 to start as $\{1,2,3,4,5\}$. $NP_1 = \{1\}$. Site 1 polls 2 which has $P_2 = \{1,2,3,4,5\}$. NP_1 becomes $\{1,2\}$ and P_1 stays the same. Now 1 polls 3 which has a $P_3 = \{1,2,3,4\}$. Site 3 can be added to NP_1 but P_1 must be changed to exclude site 5. Now site 4 is polled and P_4 is $\{1,2,4,5\}$. Site 4 cannot be added to NP_1 because it did not have all NP_1 in its partition set (i.e. it did not include site 3). Thus NP_1 is finalized to $\{1,2,3\}$ and is announced to the other sites.

Translating this algorithm into a working protocol requires provisions for synchronization and failure recovery. These two requirements make the protocol intrinsically complex because they are antagonistic: while the algorithm requires that only one active site poll for a new partition, and that other sites join only one new partition, reliability considerations require that sites be able to change active sites when one fails. Since the details of the protocol are not relevant to the overall discussion, they are not included here.

5.4   The Merge Protocol

The merge procedure joins several partitions into one. It establishes new site and mount tables, and reestablishes CSSs for all the filegroups. To form the largest possible partition, the protocol must check all possible sites, including, of course, those thought to be down. In a large network, sequential polling results in a large additive delay because of the time-outs and retransmissions necessary to determine the status of the various sites. To minimize this effect, the merge strategy polls the sites asynchronously.

The algorithm itself is simple. The site initiating the protocol sends a request for information to all sites in the network. Those sites which are able respond with the information necessary for the initiating site to build the global tables. After a suitable time, the initiating site gives up on the other sites, declares a new partition, and broadcasts its composition to the world.

The algorithm is centralized and can only be run at one site, and a site can only participate in one protocol at a time, so the other sites must be able to halt execution of the protocol. To accomplish this, the polled site sends back an error message instead of a normal reply. If a site is not ready to merge, then either it or some other site will eventually run the merge protocol.

The major source of delay in the merge procedure is in the time-out routines that decide when the full partition has answered. A fixed-length time-out long enough to handle a sizable network would add unreasonable delay to a smaller network or a small partition of a large network. The strategy used must be flexible enough to handle the large partition case and the small partition case at the same time.

The merge protocol waits longer when there is a reasonable expectation that further replies will arrive. When a site answers the poll, it sends its partition information in the reply. Until all sites believed up by some site in the new partition have replied, the time-out is long. Once all such sites have replied, the time-out is short.

5.5   The Cleanup Procedure

Even before the partition has been reestablished, there is considerable work that each node can do to clean up its internal data structures. Essentially, each machine, once it has decided that a particular site is unavailable, must invoke failure handling for all resources which its processes were using at that site, or for all local resources which processes at that site were using. The action to be taken depends on the nature of the resource and the actions that were under way when failure occurred. The cases are outlined in the table below.

After the machines in a partition have agreed upon the membership of the partition and cleaned up from site failures, the system must select, for each mounted filegroup, a new CSS. Once selected, that site must reconstruct the open file table from the information remaining in the partition.

5.6   Protocol Synchronization

The reconfiguration procedure breaks down into three distinct components, each of which has already been discussed. What remains is a discussion of how the individual parts are tied together into a robust whole. At various points in the procedure, the participating sites must be synchronized, and control of the protocol must be handed to a centralized site. Those sites not directly involved in the activity must be able to ascertain the status of the active sites to ensure that no failures have stalled the entire network.

Local Resource in Use Remotely (SS view)

Resource	Failure Action
File (open for update)	Discard pages, close file and abort updates
File (open for read)	Close file

Remote Resource in Use Locally (US view)

Resource	Failure Action
File (open for update)	Discard pages, set error in local file descriptor
File (open for read)	Internal close, attempt to reopen at other site
Terminal (read or write)	Abort read or write

Interacting Processes

Failure Type	Action
Remote Fork/Exec, remote site fails	Return error to caller
Fork/Exec, calling site fails	Abort local process
Child site dies	Parent is signalled
Parent site dies	Child inherited by local init process

One way to synchronize the sites would be to require each site to signal its readiness before beginning a new phase. This approach increases both the message traffic and the delay, both critical performance quantities. It also requires careful analysis of the critical sections in the protocols to determine where synchronization is required. If a site fails during a synchronization stage, the system must still detect and recover from that failure.

LOCUS reconfiguration extends its failure detection mechanism to handle synchronization as well. Whenever a site takes on a passive role in a protocol, it checks periodically on the active site. If the active site fails, the passive site can restart the protocol.

As the various protocols execute, the states of both the active and the passive sites change. An active site at one instant may well become a passive site the next, and a passive site could easily end up waiting for another passive site. Without adequate control, this could lead to circular waits and deadlocks.

One solution would be to have passive sites respond to the checks by returning the site that they themselves are waiting for. The checking site would then follow that chain and make sure that it terminated. This approach could require several messages per check, however, and communications delays could make the information collected obsolete or misleading.

Another alternative, the one used in LOCUS, is to order all the stages of the protocol. When a site checks another site, that site returns its own status information. A site can wait only for those sites that are executing a portion of the protocol that precedes its own. If the two sites are in the same state, the ordering is by site number. This ordering of the sites is complete. The lowest ordered site has no site to legally wait for; if it is not active, its check will fail, and the protocol can be restarted at a reasonable point.

5.7 Summary

The difficulties involved in dynamically reconfiguring an operating system are both intrinsic to the problem and dependent on the particular system. Rebuilding open file tables and synchronizing processes running in separate environments are problems of inherent difficulty. Most of the system-dependent problems can be avoided, however, with careful design.

The fact that LOCUS uses specialized protocols for operating-system-to-operating-system communication made it possible to control message traffic quite selectively. The ability to alter specific protocols to simplify the reconfiguration solution was particularly appreciated.

The task of developing a protocol by which sites would agree about the membership of a partition proved to be surprisingly difficult. Balancing the needs of protocol synchronization and failure detection while maintaining good performance presented a considerable challenge. Since reconfiguration software is run precisely when the network is unreliable, those problems are real, and not events that are unlikely.

Nevertheless, it has been possible to design and implement a solution that exhibits reasonably high performance.

6 Heterogeneity

LOCUS provides for transparent support of heterogeneous environments in two ways. First, LOCUS is machine independent in a manner similar to Unix. Moving, or "porting" LOCUS to another machine type requires little more effort than a Unix port, and sometimes less, because the system software is organized for easy retargeting to new hardware environments. The system is written almost entirely in the high-level language C. Machine dependencies are isolated by the software organization, and there exist libraries of various machine-dependent functions which can be selected at system generation time to suit the target machine.

Second, it is possible to configure a transparent LOCUS network out of computers with differing configurations and even different CPU instruction sets. Each machine in the network runs LOCUS, and the full LOCUS functionality is available throughout the net. Below, each of these facilities for handling heterogeneity is discussed in more detail.

6.1 Machine-Independent Architecture and Implementation

Aside from a small amount of machine-dependent assembly language code in the operating system kernel, all LOCUS software is written in C and must obey the strict typing rules enforced by the C type checker *lint*. As a result, machine dependencies are minimized, and the same source code is used in all versions of LOCUS, regardless of CPU type or configuration. Internally, those modules which are machine dependent by nature (e.g., memory management support) are segregated. In certain cases, of which memory management is an important example, the LOCUS source code contains a library of different algorithms, which can be selected via conditional compilation to match the hardware architecture of the target machine.

A port of LOCUS to a new machine is especially simplified if a high-quality Unix port is already available on that hardware. A LOCUS port involves essentially the same steps as a Unix port; i.e., a C compiler is needed, device drivers must be written, memory management must be built, initialization software is required, applications software must be converted if there are machine dependencies, and some kernel modification may be necessary. In addition to being Unix compatible at the application level, LOCUS maintains standard Unix interfaces inside the kernel in important cases: the device driver, memory management, and boot interfaces in particular. As a result, most of an existing

Unix port is relevant, and it is only necessary to reintegrate those modules into the LOCUS kernel that are machine dependent.

6.2   Heterogeneous Hardware in a LOCUS Network

There are three primary hardware differences relevant to a transparent software facility:

a. Configuration differences — more or less memory, the presense or absence of various peripherals (e.g., printers, graphics devices, mass storage), floating point hardware, and so forth.

b. CPU instruction set differences — since different CPUs support different instruction sets, a load module for one machine type cannot be executed by another.

c. Data format differences — different CPUs may also represent their data in a different form. As a result, both binary and text data may not be directly interchangeable among programs compiled for different CPU types, although in special cases compatibility may permit direct exchange. Within this subject we include ascii/ebcdic issues, integer length differences, different word and long word byte orders, floating point representations, etc.

Below, we outline the facilities present in the LOCUS architecture to deal with these hardware heterogeneity issues.

6.3   The LOCUS Kernel in a Heterogeneous CPU Network

In order to allow the LOCUS kernel to be distributed across sites with differing CPU types, it is necessary to handle differences in data representation between the different CPUs in the network. These differences include character sets and variations of byte ordering in integer data larger than one byte. Since the LOCUS kernel makes no use of floating point data, the issue of floating point data representation does not arise at the kernel level.

6.3.1   Byte, Word and Long Word Order

All relevant machines are assumed to have a natural byte order. Bytes are numbered from 0 (byte 0, byte 1, byte 2, etc.). The natural byte order on a machine is the order in which bytes will be accessed when byte string or sequential byte accessing instructions are used. All currently known machines generally write bytes to tape and disk in natural byte order. Also, network hardware usually preserves the natural byte order when transferring data. This leaves strings in the proper order and integer data potentially misordered. If the network hardware does not preserve natural byte order, but rather transfers data on a word-by-word basis, byte strings will be received incorrectly, but word integer data will be correct. Long integer data may still be received out of order.

Word data items (two-byte integers) may have one of two byte orders; the least significant byte comes either first or second.

Long word data items (four-byte integers) may likewise have one of two word orders; the least-significant word comes either first or second. This ordering is independent of the ordering of bytes within word data, producing four possible orderings for long word data.

6.3.2   Heterogeneous Kernel Data Exchange

There are several kernel data objects that must be transferred between sites in a LOCUS network. These include netmsgs (the standard LOCUS message header), network reconfiguration messages, update propagation messages, pages of directory files, and process states.

Whenever LOCUS transfers kernel data objects between heterogeneous sites, those objects must have their byte order restored to that of the receiver. The format of all kernel intermachine data transfers is known, and the LOCUS kernel contains procedures to transform the byte order of all messages.

In order to facilitate this transformation, all data structures that are transferred between sites in a LOCUS network are carefully laid out to guarantee that the offset and size of each element of the message and the overall message size are identical on all CPU types.

There are several questions to be answered involving byte-ordering of LOCUS kernel messages. One is to decide which site will correct the data formats. Outgoing messages are not flipped to the receiver's order. Nor does LOCUS convert network messages to a canonical byte order, in the belief that much message traffic will be among like machines. Therefore, whenever a message is transmitted from one site to another, it is sent as it is stored locally and is tagged to indicate what its byte order is. The receiver immediately uses this information along with knowledge of the structure of the message (i.e., the message type) to restore the incoming message to the native byte/word orders.

A second question is at what level in the kernel are messages reordered to the native byte order? All heterogeneous data transformations are done in the low-level, hardware-independent network driver. These transformations happen before any higher level kernel code is presented with the message, minimizing the amount of code that must be aware of heterogeneous CPUs. (The only other place such knowledge exists in the network process code to ensure that a load module is executed only on a site that has the proper CPU type.)

The final question is how do byte and word ordering differences affect the computation of the checksums required by less sophisticated network hardware? Since it is desirable to validate the checksum before any further processing (such as byte flipping) is done, order-dependent checksums are avoided. LOCUS uses only byte-wide checksums in order to prevent byte ordering from affecting the code that computes and compares checksums.

6.3.3 User Program Access to Binary System Files

All Unix systems contain certain binary databases (e.g., /etc/utmp, which records current logins). In order to allow programs to read these files, the standard interface routines provided in the C library have been extended to detect ordering and automatically transform the data to the native order before presenting it to the application program. For databases that have no standard access routines, LOCUS provides them, and they restore native byte order. Of course, programs that do not use the access routines and access binary data written by a heterogeneous CPU will read incorrect data. Similar access routines exist for directories, but since the kernel needs to use directory data, it has already been reordered by the time the user-level code receives it, and no transformation is necessary.

6.3.4   User Program Access to Remote Device Data

Data from remote devices accessed via the network is presented to the user-level program in natural byte order, since nothing is known about the structure of that data.

6.4   Hidden Directories

There are a number of situations where it is desirable for a single filesystem pathname to map to multiple files, with the choice of which file is intended made automatically as a function of the system state. One of the most common cases concerns executable load module files. When a program issues an exec call giving the name /bin/cat, it is essential that the cat command be executed. However, since we wish to support multiple CPU types in the same LOCUS network, there may be multiple load modules for cat, one for each machine type, and the system should choose the correct one. However, despite the need to map one name to multiple files under normal use, it is also necessary to be able to access any specific version of the load module file individually (e.g., when it is to be replaced with a new version).

Associating a group of files together in a way that permits individual access is done by a mechanism already present in the filesystem: the directory. What is necessary to add is a means by which such a directory of related load modules is normally hidden from view. This facility is present in LOCUS, and such directories are called *hidden directories*. The hidden directory mechanism is illustrated in the following example.

Consider a directory, /bin, containing four load module files, /bin/x, /bin/y, /bin/z, and /bin/cat. Normally, these would be plain load module files. However, assume that it was necessary to support multiple versions of the load module file /bin/cat, say one for the DEC VAX and one for the Motorola 68000. This support could be accomplished by making /bin/cat a hidden directory and installing the load modules as /bin/cat/VAX and /bin/cat/68k.

Under normal conditions, the hidden directory for cat is not visible. A reference to /bin/cat will automatically "slide through" the hidden directory and select the "appropriate" load module. This selection is controlled by per-process information which is settable with a LOCUS-specific system call.

Hidden directories are simply standard directories that are normally hidden from view. The normal "slide through" selection can be inhibited by appending the special character '@' to the hidden directory name. In the example above, /bin/cat would normally select the load module for the local machine type, but /bin/cat@ defeats the hidden "sliding through" feature and refers to the hidden directory itself, so that /bin/cat@/68k specifies the 68k load module file.

The use of an extension to the standard directory mechanism for the needed grouping function has a number of advantages, especially when compared with the alternative of constructing a new mechanism. For example, MVS is an operating system that does not provide a general hierarchical file naming structure; only one-level disk volume directories are standard. Partitioned data sets are available, however, which contain their own internal directories and therefore subfiles. However, special software is necessary to access those subfiles; the standard dataset facilities don't work. By contrast, complete compatibility is available in LOCUS for access to files in hidden directories and all standard Unix tools are available to operate on LOCUS hidden directories.

Note that load module selection is done on the basis of the *name* in the hidden directory. Programs use the *sethpath* system call to establish a list of hidden directory name entries (the hidden directory path). When a pathname search encounters a hidden directory, the LOCUS kernel searches the hidden directory once for each of the names in the hidden directory path and selects the first entry that matches. Once a selection is made, the system will still check load module type information to assure that no attempt is made to execute a load module on a mismatched machine.

While the hidden directory mechanism is a good solution to the heterogeneous CPU load module problem, it introduces some problems of its own. These problems revolve around the illusion that a hidden directory is a single file, when in fact it is a collection of several files.

In order to minimize these problems, some restrictions on the use and access of hidden directories are imposed by the LOCUS kernel. These restrictions are intended to prevent the use of hidden directories in ways not related to the support of heterogeneous load modules.

The major restriction on a hidden directory is that it must appear as a terminal node in the filesystem tree (a "leaf"). This restriction is enforced by allowing only plain files to exist inside a hidden directory; other directories and symbolic links are forbidden. There are also specific restrictions on certain system calls, as applied to hidden directories. For example, a process may not change its current working directory to be in a hidden directory.

As another example, a create cannot be done using the hidden directory name -- a component name must be specified. Additionally, one may wish to restrict and enhance system programs like *cp, mv, rm,* and *ld* to be cognizant of hidden directories.

6.5 Automatic Execution Site Selection

When a request is made to execute a program (i.e., an *exec* or *run* call is made), and the program specified for execution can run only on a machine type different from that of the machine from which the call was issued, it is usually desirable for the system to cause execution at an appropriate site automatically, in a manner transparent to the caller. So, for example, if a process executing on a VAX requests execution of a program for which the only available load module must execute on a 370, the system should invoke a transparent "remote exec" to a 370 site. LOCUS provides for this facility in a manner that may be tailored by the user. The mechanism makes use of the hidden directory facility described earlier, type information in the filesystem, per-process environment control information that is settable by the user, and the network process functions. Each of these facilities has been described earlier; we just show here how they are assembled to achieve the desired effect.

When an *exec* call is issued, the kernel uses the list of hidden directory names in the process environment to select a load module to execute. If a load module is found, the exec goes ahead as usual, checking information in the load module to ascertain which type of processor must execute it. The site of execution is the first site of the correct type on the execution site list in the process environment. When a suitable execution site is found, the LOCUS migration feature of the *exec* call is internally invoked.

6.6   Summary

LOCUS provides a basic set of facilities to deal with hardware heterogeneity. It is of course not possible to entirely hide the differences among environments, but the available facilities within LOCUS form a basis for transparently integrating a collection of highly dissimilar computers while hiding most of the unwanted machine differences from the user.

7 System Configuration, Installation, and Administration

LOCUS is relatively unique in its transparent distributed services for its users. This environment, together with the relatively low cost of remote operations results in a great deal of flexibility in configuration of a LOCUS network. The first section of this chapter indicates some of the available system configuration options and their impact. Most of these options become available only when several LOCUS sites are joined in a network, but this discussion is not meant to overlook the value of LOCUS as a single-site Unix system. Even as a single-site system, LOCUS provides features (like atomic commit and job control) to its users.

After outlining the options available in configuring LOCUS networks, LOCUS installation procedures are discussed. Installation of a single site-system and the joining or merging of additional sites are covered. Although the installation of different machine types may vary slightly in details, the general discussion applies to any LOCUS site.

The last section of this chapter addresses a few other system administration issues, especially local autonomy. The need for each site to operate and control its own resources independent of other sites in the network is accommodated by a family of tools. Of course, in order to form a LOCUS network, there must be a certain amount of cooperation and trust among the network nodes. The discussion addresses several issues of local autonomy in the day-to-day operation of a LOCUS site and network.

7.1 System Configuration

Many of the configuration issues of a LOCUS network also exist in a standard Unix system.

Considerations in configuring a Unix system include:

a. Number of users
b. Type and characteristics of user load
c. Response and delay requirements
d. Amount of disk space required
e. Number of disk arms
f. Reliability and availability issues
g. Growth potential

In order to understand how these considerations exist in a LOCUS picture, consider User X, logged into Site A and using Site B to store his files. As User X goes about his work he will generate disk traffic on Site B and network traffic between Sites A and B. The response User X experiences depend on the presented load at both Sites A and B and the disk he is using on Site B. In one model of a LOCUS network, Site A is a personal workstation and provides relatively constant response to User X. The performance, however, is affected by the the load presented to the disk on Site B by other users sharing that resource.

The above discussion outline is intended to illustrate how issues in configuring a LOCUS network are just a superset of the issues on a single-site Unix system. New issues result from the opportunities that transparent distributed operation provides. These issues stem largely from the topology of the LOCUS network and the amount of real sharing among the network users.

7.1.1 Time-sharing Topology

One possible topology for a LOCUS network is a set of nodes, each providing time-sharing services to its users. The degree of sharing among the sites will depend on the type of load presented and how the network is administered. If some class of users may log into more than one node, then those users will see increased availability. If the machines are administered collectively, a reduced staff is required to support the collection of machines because of the transparency provided by LOCUS.

7.1.2 Front End Processor Topology

In a front end processor topology, the mainframes composing the backbone of the network are surrounded by some number of reasonably fast but small computers. These are the front end processors and are real LOCUS nodes, but may have little or no disk space. Users access the main hosts through these front ends, to which most terminals are connected. The front ends provide interactive services to the users, but the site of execution is fully transparent. This topology has the advantages of allowing the backbone sites to provide the cpu-intensive functions and file service, and putting terminal-intensive operations in a machine with a relatively fixed load close to the user.

In this model a modest investment in the front ends results in what could easily be substantial improvement in user-perceived performance and host throughput. The transparency of LOCUS permits the administrator to set up the hosts so that any editor will be run on front end processors transparently to the user. While the user is in the editor session, he will interact only with the front end. Greater efficiency can be achieved in this way than by running an editor directly on a main backbone site — many Unix (LOCUS) editors run in raw mode and, therefore, wakeup the editor process for each character typed. During the front end editor session, the front end may communicate with a main site providing temporary file service. When the user is done, his exit writes out the file back to the appropriate host.

The two topologies outlined both move LOCUS service closer to the user. The next natural step is to dedicate a LOCUS workstation node to each individual user. This topology is described below.

7.1.3 Workstation Topology

In a workstation topology each user has a workstation that he uses when he needs service. The workstation may be on the user's desk or nearby in a pool of workstations. The advantage of this model is that the user is in control of his own service for those things that he can do on the workstation. If the hosts go down, the user may continue working if he is using files and services on his workstation. When the host is present, the user may transparently put long-running, cpu-intensive tasks on the hosts. In this model the user has complete freedom and is bounded only by the protection framework of the system.

In some environments the system users might not demand enough load to require a LOCUS node on their desks, but when they do want to use the system they may desire the workstation model. One solution to this problem is to have a pool of workstations used by several people. In this situation it would probably be best for the users to store some or all of their files on the host, since which workstation a user employs may change, and file service from the main hosts is likely to be superior to that from a workstation other than the one currently employed by the user. They are then not bound to use a particular workstation and will contend only when the entire workstation pool is in use. In order to get back the freedom of independent operation, they need only move copies of the currently interesting files to their workstations.

7.1.4   Replication Considerations

The LOCUS system provides system support for replication of user files. The degree of replication is controlled by the user after the system administrators provide the disk space for the copies and enable the protection controls for the user. Exactly where the copies of a filesystem should exist and which site should be the primary copy are clearly issues that need to be addressed during system configuration. The administrators should consider at least the following issues:

a. Update rate of the files
b. Probable location of the updating processes
c. CPU load of the primary site
d. Read access rate of the files and their location
e. Performance issues (network load)
f. Reliability and availability issues
g. Growth potential

Configuration of user filesystems is one area where specific installation experience would be useful. As an example, the conditions under which it makes sense for the user to have a replicated filesystem on his workstation with the workstation being the primary copy depends on site reliability, the frequency of access from sites other than the workstation, etc.

We now turn from the configuration of a network to the installation of LOCUS sites and related issues.

7.2   LOCUS Installation

The set of installation decisions involved in a LOCUS system is a superset of those for a Unix system. A conventional Unix system permits one to set such parameters as the number of filesystem buffers, the size of kernel tables, etc. Tools are provided to partition disks into separate filesystems and initialize them. Further, because LOCUS can be a network system, there are additional configuration choices that involve the organization of LOCUS nodes operating together in the net.

Lastly, it is highly desirable to be able to convert easily from a conventional Unix system to a LOCUS system, either to join a LOCUS network, or to continue operating as a single site, but with enhanced functionality.

7.2.1 LOCUS Installation Philosophy

In this section, we discuss the options available during installation of a LOCUS system, and outline the general principles followed by the installation software. The LOCUS installation tools are designed to make default installations of LOCUS systems as simple as possible, with the eventual goal to have a system completely install itself. In addition, individual configuration choices are available to sophisticated users so that they may alter any given subset of default decisions. The various installation options are discussed below, followed by an outline of the installation software architecture.

7.2.2 Conversion of a Unix System to LOCUS

Replacement of a Unix system by LOCUS is designed to be a straightforward operation. It may vary slightly across different machine types depending on the characteristics of the Unix system being replaced. For example, it may nor may not be possible to convert user file systems in place. The important consideration is whether the resulting LOCUS filesystem will fit in the same space allocated for the Unix filesystem. The basic system conversion procedure is outlined below:

a. If the filesystems can not be converted in place, then save the user filesystems on backup medium using cpio(1) and run *LocusFit* to be sure that filesystems will fit after conversion.

b. Save the system-related disk areas (root filesystem, etc.) using cpio(1).

c. Read in the distribution system from tape or diskette. The distribution includes a generic root filesystem and local filesystem.

d. Boot the distribution LOCUS system and run the configuration program *GoLocus*. *GoLocus* will convert the generic distribution system into the specific system being installed.

e. Configure the LOCUS system appropriately for the cpu and I/O devices to be used. After installing the newly configured LOCUS kernel, reboot the system.

f. Convert the user filesystems to LOCUS format using *LOCUSConvert*, or restore user filesystems from backup if necessary.

This procedure converts the Unix system to a LOCUS system by entirely replacing the Unix kernel and associated system software (all of the root file system). Restoration of user filesystems, rather than conversion in place to LOCUS filegroups, may be necessary because the LOCUS disk image contains more information for each file than Unix does, and there is no assurance that the block size used for LOCUS filegroups matches that of the conventional Unix system being replaced.

This standard conversion procedure will require user intervention if the system being replaced is not a standard Unix system, but rather one that has kernel or system program alterations upon which the user's software depends. In that case, it will be necessary for the user to save his old root filesystem before conversion also, and restore it as some other named filesystem, so that files from it can be accessed under LOCUS, and necessary changes integrated.

Some LOCUS systems may also require slightly more disk storage than their conventional Unix counterparts to hold the same set of files. Therefore, if a given Unix file system is completely full, it may not restore successfully under LOCUS. In that case, it is necessary to archive some files first before conversion.

7.2.3 Merging Unix Sites to become a LOCUS System

To merge separate existing Unix systems into an integrated LOCUS network, several steps are required. First, the primary site for the replicated root should be selected and converted to a single-site LOCUS system, as described above. Then, certain agreements need to be established regarding:

    a. User names and uids, group names and gids
    b. Global filesystem numbers
    c. Site names
    d. File naming hierarchy
    e. Replication plan
    f. Local autonomy controls

Each of these issues is discussed below. Some actions are prerequisites for joining sites together. Other steps can be taken incrementally, at least in part, while the integrated system is in operation. Assuming these issues have been resolved, the conversion and merging is completed as follows:

Perform steps a and b from the single-site conversion procedure.

a. Using the distribution tools, install a local filesystem and an empty root filesystem.

b. Boot the LOCUS distribution and bring it up on the network. The system will propagate a root filesystem to the new site.

c. Perform steps d and e from the single-site conversion procedure to configure the I/O devices.

d. Use step f from the single-site conversion procedure to restore the site's user filesystems.

As indicated above there are a number of issues that must be resolved in merging several Unix sites into a single LOCUS network. Many of these are also issues in merging several LOCUS sites or networks into a single LOCUS network. These issues are now addressed.

7.2.3.1 User Names and Uids, Group Names and Gids

An integrated system requires that all user and group names, as well as the internal system user and group ids (uids and gids) be globally unique. It is the system administrators' responsibility to decide, in the case of conflict, what user or group names should be altered and what they will become. This change can be done on the individual systems before joining, or in the process of converting the user filesystems. Then it is necessary for the uids and gids for each system to be made different from those on all other systems being integrated.

These steps are required before the new LOCUS site can be made available on the LOCUS network. A user with accounts on different systems will end up with different accounts in the joined network. He may wish to merge them once the network is operational.

7.2.3.2 Global Filesystem Numbers

It is also necessary for each mounted filesystem to have a unique internal global logical filesystem number. In addition it is essential that each replicated copy of a filesystem have a pack number distinct from all other copies. A simple utility is provided to set the global filesystem number and pack number. It is the system administrators' responsibility to assure that all filesystem numbers are unique.

7.2.3.3 Site Names

LOCUS requires that all site names and internal site numbers be unique. When bringing up a site, it is straightforward to select the site name and number. The network reconfiguration software will object if an attempt is made to add a site with the same name and/or number as an already existing site. Site numbers are not registered, however, so it is possible to have a duplicate number with a site that is currently down. The file */etc/site* contains a mapping of site name to internal site number as well as other information relevant to the site.

7.2.3.4 File Naming Hierarchy

LOCUS provides a highly convenient, global naming environment for all users. The value of this environment is discussed in early chapters of this document. However, when joining a set of existing systems, some work may be necessary if those systems have been operating with conflicting naming hierarchies. This issue arises when a set of systems have altered pathnames and filesystem names from the standard Unix tree structure, especially if those alterations have occurred near the top of the naming hierarchy. As a frequent example, one site may have put all new programs from U.C. Berkeley in /ucb/bin, while another may have just merged them into /bin. This case, where two sets of names have been used for the same set of files, is not really a problem. Both copies can be kept initially, in different global filesystems, and storage can be recovered later during normal LOCUS operation by constructing links, or by changing programs that depend on one set of names.

A more difficult case occurs when the same name is used for different objects. This case is not too common in system software, since the practice which leads to it also inhibits software interchange among systems. Nevertheless, it is possible.

The issue also arises in another way: when two different sites have different versions of the same program — an old and new version of a compiler, for example.

The preferable solution is to make a choice regarding which name, or set of paths, or program version will be the one used. The other program can be named *program.old,* or the other directory called *dir.site1*, for example.

The file hierarchy for user filesystems may also conflict. For example user files for two sites may be under the */u* directory. By either integrating the users' directories into one filesystem or changing to distinct hierarchies for both sites this problem can be solved.

7.2.3.5 Filesystem Layout and Replication Plan

LOCUS permits considerable flexibility in configuring storage and peripherals. For example, one could choose to provide large amounts of storage at certain high-performance machines in the network to provide substantial file service to workstations with little or no local secondary store. In a large network configuration, these choices involve significant technical evaluations of network bandwidth, disk capacity and bandwidth, etc. While LOCUS does not automatically answer such questions, it permits any reasonable configuration, and permits alterations to be made sometime after system installation in order to optimize system behavior, without affecting any application software.

Since LOCUS permits replication of any filegroup, one must decide which filegroups are to be replicated, and where in the network copies will be located. It is necessary to replicate the root filegroup at all sites for which independent operation is desired. In addition, enough copies of the root should be allocated so that all sites not storing the root will be assured that *some* copy will be available at all times. Any additional copies are needed only for performance considerations.

For other filegroups, the choice of degree of replication is largely a user concern, not related to system operation. The considerations are availability and performance, as discussed earlier. In every case of a replicated filegroup, one site needs to be designated as both the default current synchronization site (CSS) and primary site (PS). That site where the plurality of accesses are to be made is preferred, to minimize network traffic.

Once a filegroup allocation plan has been established, laying out the filegroups is straightforward using LOCUS extensions to standard Unix utility software.

7.2.3.6 Peripherals

LOCUS provides a high degree of transparent access to peripheral devices in an integrated network. Full transparency is provided for all block devices and all terminals. Unix "raw" devices may be accessed by invoking the calling process at the device site.

Since many of the devices of interest may be transparently accessed, the number of specialized devices, such as printers, tape drives, foreign network gateways, etc., can often be reduced. Where such devices should be attached in the network can then largely be based on performance, load, and availability considerations. These issues are typical system manager decisions; LOCUS merely permits substantial freedom in making and changing them.

7.2.4 Adding New CPU Types

The discussion above outlined the procedures for installing a single-site LOCUS system as well as for merging multiple Unix sites into a LOCUS network. It was implied that these machines were of the same cpu type, but LOCUS also supports heterogeneous operation within a single network. The procedure for adding a node of a different machine is similar to that outlined for merging two Unix sites. Assume that the primary site of the root file system is operational and has binaries for the new type of processor. To add the new LOCUS site, simply follow the procedure outlined for adding another site of the same type as the primary site. If the primary site does not have the binaries for the new site, then it will be necessary to add them. Adding the binaries to the primary site may involve increasing the size of the root filesystem. Where possible, LOCUS distributions take this requirement into account and provide either the binaries in the root or adequate storage space.

7.2.5 Merging Two LOCUS Networks

In order to merge two LOCUS networks, it is necessary to select one of the two primary sites for the root file system to become the primary site of the resulting network. Alternatively, some other site could be selected. After such a selection the procedure for merging two Unix sites into a LOCUS network can be followed to produce the single

LOCUS network. In this case there will be no requirement to convert the format of the users' filesystems, although the issues concerning uids and gids will still exist.

7.2.6 Summary

Most of the steps outlined in this section are quite straightforward. The only complex issues are establishing naming hierarchy agreement and planning replication. The former can be done in stages during routine operation of the integrated distributed system, as pointed out in the earlier discussion. The latter is little different from the kind of site storage decisions required in any significant system installation.

For a conventional installation of new LOCUS nodes, a default set of configuration decisions have been made, and an automatic, bootable distribution form of LOCUS is available.

7.3 System Administration

The administration of a LOCUS network will vary depending on its topology and the characteristics of the user population. Many of the issues concerning a Unix site remain key issues for LOCUS and can be dealt with as they were for the Unix system. One issue which requires some discussion, local autonomy, is addressed below.

7.3.1 Local Autonomy

The LOCUS architecture integrates a set of computing engines into a single logical system. In some situations the entire collection of machines can be considered as a single machine from an administrative standpoint. In other cases, however, different groups or individuals will have responsibility for resources in the system and will wish to have control over those resources.

In a standard Unix system, resource control is accomplished by a combination of owner/group protections, setuid superuser programs, and access to the superuser account (to which the kernel affords special privileges). In a network, a single superuser account either should be eliminated, or the need for access to it should be severely limited. Multiple superuser accounts are not sufficient to get the resource control needed.

In LOCUS, the approach to providing decentralized control over resources is handled by a set of facilities. First, existing conventional Unix protection facilities are preserved and used to control access to files. Second, a number of *control functions* are provided for use in a decentralized manner. Those functions are typically found in existing setuid-superuser software. Those programs have been altered in LOCUS to interrogate a new, simple user control database to decide whether to allow the requested action. That database thus permits one, for each setuid-superuser program, to give various users (administrators, for example) tools to manage resources under their control. In addition, a few other setuid-superuser programs have been created, which also interrogate that same user database and provide additional resource control tools. Third, there are a variety of *data objects* whose update should be controlled in a more decentralized manner than, for example, the Unix file protection facilities provide. In most cases, access to them is handled by a simple copy program, giving the privileged user a version that can be updated by any preferred standard tools and then copied back. This special copy program also interrogates the user database mentioned above.

With these facilities, it is rarely necessary to exercise superuser privileges. For example, consider the *kill* program, which is used to terminate tasks. In standard Unix, *kill* is only able to terminate tasks belonging to the user who invokes it. To terminate anyone else's tasks, the invoker of *kill* must be the superuser. In LOCUS, the *kill* utility has been extended to check the user database to decide whether a request to terminate a given process will be allowed to succeed. By this means, individual managers (or faculty) can be given the ability to control resource usage by their direct employees (or students), without giving a particular manager the ability to terminate tasks belonging to members of other departments.

Another example is the *adduser* program, which permits changing the password file, including adding accounts and setting which sites in the network the account can use, all in a decentralized manner. A given administrator may be given the ability to add accounts, but only empowered with the ability to execute on a small subset of sites in the LOCUS network.

Further, a given installation can extend these facilities by adding to the user database and/or providing additional resource control software tools that also use the database.

In general, decentralization of resource control and protection decisions is mandatory because there is a *large* set of cooperating users in the network. This approach is the same whether the set of users is executing on a single mainframe (as in a community of several thousand people sharing a large Amdahl computer), or on a network of workstations. It should also be noted that this problem cannot be solved satisfactorily by constructing barriers to transparency (as advocated by some who would operate workstations largely as stand-alone machines), since the need to cooperate in reasonable ways always leads to methods by which individuals can abuse available resources in the network. (Consider for example sending users mail to fill their disks.)

The detailed list of resource control programs and their options continues to evolve as the system matures. As further operational experience is obtained, additional programs no doubt will be added.

7.4 Summary

In this chapter some of the configuration, installation, and administration issues in a LOCUS network have been addressed. In the early design phases of LOCUS, it was assumed that most operations would be done on the site local to the resources. Experience with LOCUS networks since their construction has indicated that as a result of the excellent remote performance users do not worry about the location of the resources, but instead operate on the least-loaded cpu in the network. In fact at one LOCUS beta site, a simple load-leveling application called *nomad* was constructed. *Nomad* was a background task the user started up when he logged into the system. Its function was to wake up every few minutes and verify that the user's shell was running on the least loaded site. If it was not, then a migrate signal was sent to the shell and it moved to the least loaded site *without the user's intervention.*

The remote operations are not without their costs. Even though remote performance is comparable to local performance, more system cycles are expended by sites in the network to perform a remote operation than a local operation. Consider the case of reading a page, for example. Whether the page is local or remote, the disk page is still read. If the page is stored on another site, then it must be sent through the network in addition to being read off the disk. This means that remote operations consume more of the total cpu cycles in the network than local operations. This point is not meant to discourage remote operations, nor to inhibit users from taking advantage of the transparency provided by LOCUS, but rather to help administrators understand the LOCUS system and its configuration to a fuller extent.

LOCUS is a relatively young system and therefore the impacts of the various configuration trade-offs are not totally understood. As more installations occur and administrators start to experiment with the configuration flexibility that LOCUS provides, a better understanding of the configuration management will result.

8 Conclusions

The transparency provided by LOCUS can be viewed as having several principal components: files, peripheral devices, and processes. The transparent file system is widely used, and its value is emphasized by the substantial number of other systems which provide some form of transparent, remote file access. Limited forms of remote file access are reasonably straightforward to build, as well. (However, *location transparency* is difficult, since it requires some form of replicated catalogs.) Remote peripheral access, to the degree that the behavior can be fit into the file system, is also quite feasible. Transparent tasking, however, is a more sophisticated function. To provide it, one must first have transparent file and device access, since otherwise, when a task moves, the environment in which it executes will have changed, and the result will not be transparent. Without transparent tasking, though, such functions as load leveling, high availability services, automatic selection of appropriate machine types, etc. are exceedingly difficult to provide.

The clearest conclusion to be drawn from the LOCUS work is that transparency is both feasible and highly desirable in a network environment. Perspectives gained during development and use are detailed below. The choice of Unix as a base is also reviewed, and some comments regarding future work are made.

8.1 Experiences

A number of conclusions can be drawn from the use of a highly transparent system like LOCUS. They are outlined below.

First, of course, transparency in all of its dimensions, is exceedingly valuable. Both name and location transparency, as discussed in Chapter two, are needed. The ease with which distributed applications, such as data management, load leveling, and simple sharing of information among users of different machines and workstations in a LOCUS network are achieved, is very satisfying. It is really feasible to have most of the advantages of a personal workstation, for example, while at the same time retaining the logical simplicity provided by resource and information sharing on a single timesharing system.

Users of transparent systems inevitably conclude that to give up transparency is unthinkable, just as one wouldn't consider abandoning virtual memory in favor of writing overlay code, or giving up a screen editor in favor of a line oriented one.

Surprisingly, LOCUS also demonstrated that a significant degree of performance transparency could also be achieved, at least in suitable local network environments. This result has considerable significance, since it means that less care needs to be exercised with respect to the location of resources in the network. Difficult and complex optimization problems need not be solved.

However, one should not have the impression that providing a transparent system is without pitfalls. First of all, transparency is like compatibility. Its value is dramatically increased as remaining exceptions are removed. Unlike many other areas of computer science, it is not the case that most of the value of transparency can be achieved through a partial solution.

Most of the difficulties encountered by users with early versions of LOCUS resulted from exceptions to transparency. For example, before the token mechanism described in Chapter three was completed, "exclusive write, shared read" was the cross-machine synchronization policy for file access; i.e. if a user on one site had opened a file for write, no users on other sites could access the file at all. Some Unix programs had to be modified to operate in this environment, and distributed execution was less convenient.

Once a high degree of transparency is achieved, not surprisingly, clients make substantial use of it, and pay little attention to the location of resources; until a failure occurs, that is. The site on which the user's software was executing may be continuing normally. However, some remote site may be storing a file used by that program, without the user being aware. Nevertheless, when that site fails, his service is interrupted. The availability of service is now potentially affected by the stability of more sites, precisely because it was so easy to distribute resources.

There are two solutions to this problem. First, one can strive to assure that the availability of sites is exceedingly high. This step makes sense even in the absense of a distributed environment. Second, one can design the system architecture to take advantage of the enormous resource redundancy which is typically present in a network of workstations and mainframes. It is for this reason that the file replication facilities in

LOCUS are so valuable.

Nevertheless, on balance, the advantages of transparency, which have been addressed throughout this book, far outweigh the issues raised here.

8.2 Unix Retrospective

Unix was chosen as the base system to extend into the network transparent environment for several principal reasons. First, it was the only reasonably general purpose operating system available that was written in a high level language. That characteristic was considered important from the points of view of minimizing the difficulty of modification and the resulting independence from particular hardware. Second, the developers and users of Unix had practiced a high degree of "information hiding", in the sense that application programs rarely used any other information besides the system call interface and a few external data structures. Thus, the internals of the operating system could be altered substantially without affecting the vast majority of application software. As a result, the LOCUS developers avoided construction of virtually all non-operating system software; to do otherwise would have been a fearsome task indeed, with little to do with distributed computing.

However, as one would expect, the Unix model was not without its problems. The most significant ones were the occasional failure to practice information hiding, and aspects of the Unix process model that are not oriented for use in a distributed, non-shared memory environment.

Information hiding failures occur in several ways, principally in directory access and system data structures like /etc/utmp, etc. Directories may be read like any other file in Unix, so their detailed structure is visible, and used, by a few application software. Similarly, programs can directly read a variety of system data files, which generally differ from one machine type to another. If these data structures had been accessed via library routines for example, then one would have been able to alter them without needing to fix the affected applications; only relinking would have been necessary. The solution in LOCUS has been to provide such routines, and fix the relevant programs to use them, so that subsequent internal alterations, or machine dependent behavior, could be masked.

The Unix model for process interactions presented more intrinsic difficulties. In particular, Unix contains a substantial number of shared memory characteristics in the way processes affect one another. The file system is seen globally by all processes; any change caused by one process is immediately visible system-wide. Further, processes in the same family often share the same current file pointer. Thus, when one process reads a byte, and another reads a byte, the second should see the byte *after* the one seen by the first. As one can easily imagine, while such semantics can be provided in a straightforward way when all processes share random access memory, it is an altogether different matter in a distributed system. The issues are even further complicated by the kinds of race conditions and failures which may occur in a network. Clearly, one can design far more stylized interfaces through which processes would interact within a single machine, so that extension to a network would be far easier. Nevertheless, the utility of having provided a widely used process model in the distributed environment has been exceedingly high, since one immediately obtains substantial amounts of software that can be run without modification.

On balance, the choice of Unix was a very positive one, in good part because of the issues just discussed; but also because it is a widely enough used system that people care about extensions to it that may have utility.

8.3   Architectural Lessons

Transparency is not free. In addition to the rather substantial amount of design effort, considerable development is required, beyond what would otherwise be necessary. Further, that development can easily be deceiving. Prototypes of LOCUS were operational, providing good quality behavior under normal conditions, years before a producion quality system was complete. The reasons were the vast amount of analysis, design time, implementation effort, and quality assurance needed to provide robust behavior in the face of all manner of errors, race conditions, partial failures, etc. Until this aspect of the task is faced, one can be assured that only the first part of the job is done.

In fact, this observation is another powerful argument in favor of transparency. Experience with LOCUS has shown that, since the system must handle these problems successfully anyway, most applications are relieved of much necessity to deal with them explicitly. That is a dramatic savings.

8.4 Futures

There is still more to do. A distributed system would be materially aided by further high availability enhancements. Transaction support, in the form of networkwide two phase commit, for example, would be very valuable to have in the operating system. While versions of such a service have been built for LOCUS, they have not been integrated into the production system, and so they are not discussed in this book.

Use of transparency in networks where performance transparency cannot be provided, such as low bandwidth, long haul situations, also appears promising, but there is little experience in such a situation, so further work undoubtedly will be needed.

In fact, the distributed system era has just now begun. With the advent of highly transparent systems, it finally becomes easy to construct distributed applications. Those applications are only now beginning to be seen. The excitement and challange lies in the *use* of these systems.

Appendix A

Additional LOCUS System Calls

Below is a list of the system calls added to a standard System V or 4.1 BSD Unix kernel to allow programs to optionally interrogate or control the added functionality in LOCUS. The first set of calls are largely available to application programs (some of the *set* calls are superuser only) while the second set are used for system administrator programs

chhidden	Change hidden attribute of directory, making hidden directories from regular directories and vice versa.
commit	File changes made up to the point of the commit call are made permanent.
dfstat	Get file status of open file, including new LOCUS fields.
dstat	Extended version of stat, giving new LOCUS fields.
getcommit, setcommit	Return or change the current default (commit/abort) action to be taken when an exception occurs.
gethpath, setpath	Return or change the current hidden directory search path.
getlocal, setlocal	Return or set name of the current process's <LOCAL> filesystem.
getsites, setsites	Return which sites are in your partition or set which sites may be in your partition. Setting is restricted to superuser.
getxperm, setxperm	Return or change list of sites on which the current process is permitted to execute or have children execute. Setting is restricted to superuser.
getxsites, setxsites	Return or change the execution site list used for future fork, exec, run, and migrate calls.
kill3	Similar to kill except an additional argument is passed. This is useful to signal SIGMIGRATE where a site needs to be specified.
lmknod	Extended version of mknod, allowing the setting of the site a device resides on.
migrate	Move calling procedure to another site.
readlink	Return the filename to which a symbolic link points.

runl, runle, runv, runve   Create a new process and transfer control to it.

sabort   File changes made up to the point of the abort call after the last
                            commit are thrown away.

select   Return information on which file descriptors are ready for I/O.
                            This allows synchronous I/O multiplexing.

setxuid   Use real user id or group id for subsequent invocations of run.

site   Return the site number at which the currently running or specified
                            process is executing.

symlink   Create a symbolic link (similar to 4.2 feature).

Below is the second list, which are system calls used by system administrator functions
like filesystem reconciliation.

netstart   Initiate network activity.

probe   Validate status of a site by attempting to communicate with it.

raccept   Give me a function to perform - used to allow the kernel to have
                            processes started up (eg. filesystem reconciliation)

propv   Tell the kernel to propagate a given version of a given file.
                            Superuser only and used by filesystem reconciliation process.

chlwm   Change or interrogate the low water mark of a filegroup pack.
                            Superuser only and used by filesystem reconciliation process.

Appendix B

LOCUS Internal Network Messages

This appendix contains a description of the messages which make up the LOCUS network protocol. Each of these *request* messages, except where noted, are received by the network device interrupt routine at the destination site and added to a queue of network requests which is serviced by a pool of dedicated, lightweight kernel processes. Along with a description of each message, there is an indication of the information sent in the message and the characteristics of the message, drawn from the following:

a. *Small* (default) or *Large*: Currently all messages are either *large* or *small*. *Small* messages do not include a data page, but only the 140-byte control message. *Large* messages have both.

b. *No-response-needed* (default), *Need-small-response*, or *Need-large-response*: Certain request messages in the protocol require that a response message be sent back to the site which sent the request. Response messages carry the same message type as the request and are delivered to the requesting process when received. For each message below which requires a response, a description of the information sent in the response is also given.

c. *Ack-needed* (default) or *Noack*: A few messages do not need an acknowledgement and are so designated, allowing the device driver, which does Ack processing, to handle them properly. If a request message requires a response, either both the request and the response require an acknowledgement, or neither does.

d. *Not-special* (default) or *Special*: *Special* messages are those relating to network configuration control. Only messages marked as *special* will be processed if they come from a site not indicated as being "up." If a request message is marked *special*, then its response, if any, is special as well.

e. *Not-serviced-by-interrupt* (default) or *Serviced-by-interrupt*: *Serviced-by-interrupt* messages are those request messages for which service is simple enough and performance is important enough that the servicing can be accomplished while processing the interrupt.

The first set of messages concern the filesystem activity.

OPEN (US -> CSS; *Need-small-response*) Open or stat a file (which includes
devices). The type of the open includes READ, MOD, STAT. The filename
given is a globally unique low-level name: <global filegroup number (gfs),
inode number (inode)>. An inode value of zero indicates a request to create a
new file. If the US stores the file, it indicates which version it stores. If the
US needs a particular SS or version vector, it so indicates. Although the
messages is primarily sent from the US to the CSS, it is sent from the US to a
SS during open for propagation (PROPIN) and when stats at particular sites
are requested. If the open succeeded, the US is told, in the response, who the
SS is; if the SS is not the US, a copy of the inode is sent in the response.

BESS (CSS -> SS; *Need-small-response*) A request for this storage site to service the
OPEN request made; the <gfs,inode> is sent along with the identity of the
SS, and an indication of which version of the file is requested. If yes, the
response includes a copy of the inode.

DEVOPEN (US -> SS; *Need-small-response*) After the OPEN has succeeded, the US
can request a device open if the file is a device; the device open routine
applicable for this file will be executed; <gfs,inode> is sent with an indication
of READ or MOD; this device open action cannot be done during the OPEN
message since permission checks, etc., are done at the US after the OPEN, but
before any action to the device wants to be done.

READ (US -> SS; *Need-large-response, Noack*) Request for a page of an open file;
the logical page number is included in the message, along with the in-core
inode slot number of this already open file. The response always includes
1024 bytes of message which is the data, unless there was an error.

WRITE (US -> SS; *Large*) Request to store a page of data (which is included in the
message) of an open file; the logical page number is included in the message,
along with the in-core inode slot number of this already open file.

ERR (SS -> US) Asynchronous message indicating an error in a previous WRITE; <gfs,inode,logical page number> are sent; at the US, the in-core inode is marked with this information so that the next activity on this file gets the error; this is only a warning message since the USCLOSE or USCOMMIT messages will fail in any event.

USCLOSE (US -> SS; *Need-small-response*) Close, in the mode indicated, the open file specified by the in-core inode slot number; only sent on last close at the US; handles telling the CSS about the close if this is the last close for this SS (see SSCLOSE). Having a response avoids the race of having the US try to reopen the file before the close messages have gotten to the CSS. This message is sent only after the response to SSCLOSE has been received from the CSS.

SSCLOSE (SS -> CSS; *Need-small-response*) Close the file; the SS may have had the file open for several USs, and only on the last close is this message sent to the CSS to unlock the file and deallocate in-core resources; also sent if downgrading the open mode from MOD to READ.

CLOSESS (CSS -> SS) Requests an SS to stop serving as an SS for a particular replicated file. This message is sent when a US attempts to open a replicated file for MOD, at which time all opens for READ must use the copy of the file stored at the CSS.

CLOSEUS (SS -> US) Requests a using site to close the file. Sent to all USs when an SS receives a CLOSESS message from the CSS.

CLSFSS (SS -> US) Message from an SS to each of its USs when a change to a file is committed. The message contains the new inode and an indication of whether the content of the file changed as well, in which case each US other than the site which made the change will invalidate its buffers for this file and get the new pages from the SS as they are needed.

USCOMMIT (US -> SS; *Need-small-response*) Commit this file; sent with the in-core inode slot number of the SS inode and a new copy of the disk inode information; only sent after all pages of the file have been flushed from the US to the SS. The response is sent after the CSS and all other SSs have been notified of the change, but before all SSs have had the opportunity to propagate the new version of the file. The response indicates an error if not all the writes were done successfully.

ABORT (US -> SS; *Need-small-response*) Abort the changes made to this file; restore to the last committed version; in-core inode slot number is sent. The response includes the restored copy of the inode so the US can start afresh.

TRUNC (US -> SS) Truncate a file. The specified open file is to be truncated to the indicated length. Additional pages are deallocated. Currently, the only supported length to which a file may be truncated is 0 (making it an empty file).

FUNBLOCK (SS -> US) A pipe reader is awakened. The reader was told to sleep in the response to a prior READ message. The <gfs, inode> sent in the message is used to locate the process.

CHINODE (US -> SS; *Need-small-response*) This message is used to change an inode field of a file. File attributes such as link count, owner, and activity times can be changed and the file committed all at the SS. The response indicates success or failure.

USLOCKF (US -> SS; *Need-small-response*) A request to acquire a lock on an open file. The response indicates success or failure.

SSLOCKF (SS -> CSS; *Need-small-response*) A request to acquire a lock on an open file on behalf of a requesting US. The response indicates success or failure.

USTAT (US -> CSS; *Need-small-response*) Requests superblock information from the CSS of a specified filegroup to implement the *ustat* system call.

UPDATEPROP (CSS -> SS) Inform all other sites which store a copy of a file that a new copy of this file has been committed so they can request the changes; <gfs,inode> is sent along with the new version number of the file and a set of bits indicating which pages had changed; action is part of commit service.

REQLBNLIST (SS -> CSS; *Need-large-response*) The SS requests the CSS to respond with a large message containing the list of logical page numbers changed in the last commit.

GETCOMLIST (SS -> SS; *Need-large-response*) Request superblock commit list from one SS to another; sent during filesystem reconciliation.

The next set of messages are for both the File Offset and Data Token mechanisms which control concurrent distributed file access.

TOKINIT (US -> SS; *Need-small-response*) Set up a token control block, adding the requesting US to the list of sites which are sharing a file offset structure. The response includes the TCB descriptor used to refer to the token control block in subsequent messages.

RQSTOK (US -> SS) Request a file offset or data token; if the token is held by another US, the SS will recall it from that US using RELTOK; when the token is available it is given to the US with AWARDTOK.

AWARDTOK (SS -> US) Awards token to a US that requested it using RQSTOK.

RELTOK (SS -> US) Asks US to release a file offset or data token; the US will reply with TOKRLSD as soon as possible (possibly before receiving this message).

TOKRLSD (US -> SS) Give a file offset or data token back to the SS.

CLRTOK (US -> SS) Sent on final close at a US of a file offset structure; deallocates token control block if this was the last site sharing this file offset.

The next set of messages are for Remote Process Management.

FPR (*Large, Need-small-response*) Requesting site sends a request to do a *fork*, *migrate*, *run*, or *exec* to the site on which the execution is to occur. Included in the request is data from the requesting process's user structure and process structure. Response indicates success of failure.

SENV (*Need-large-response, Serviced-by-interrupt*) New execution site sends a series of these messages to get the argument data in the case of *exec* and *run*. This message is serviced by the process which issued the FPR message.

SPDTA (*Need-large-response, Serviced-by-interrupt*) The new execution site sends, in the case of *fork* or *migrate*, a series of these requests to get the user stack and the process data image. This message is serviced by the process which issued the FPR message.

FRKDONE (*Serviced-by-interrupt*) The new execution site sends this message to the parent site to indicate that the new process has successfully been set up, so the parent can take appropriate action (for migrate or exec, this means to terminate execution after sending an EXECDONE message).

EXECDONE (*Large, Serviced-by-interrupt*) This message is sent from the old to the new execution site of an *Exec* or *Migrate* to pass ownership of the process id, before the process on the old execution site self-destructs. Included in the message are any pending signals and a list of execution sites for each of this process's children.

WAIT (Parent -> Child; *Need-small-response*) This is sent to the site where a remote child is known to have exited to collect status information about the child.

ABANDON (Parent -> Child; *Need-small-response*) This is sent to the site where a remote child is to announce that the parent is exiting.

The next set of messages are for Process and Process Group Tracking.

PSPAR (Child -> Parent; *Need-small-response*) This message is sent from a process to the site of its parent process when it moves to another site during an *Exec* or *Migrate*.

PSORIG (Process Site -> Origin Site) This message is sent from a process to its origin site as notification that the process has moved to this site.

PSGRP (Process Site -> Group Origin Site; *Need-small-response*) This message is sent from a process to the origin site of its process group as notification that the process has moved to this site.

PSTOP (*Large*) This message is sent during network reconfiguration to pass information about remote processes executing on this site.

The next set of messages are for signaling remote processes:

SIGPROC (*Need-small-response*) Deliver a signal to a remote process. If the site on which a process is executing isn't known, the message is first sent to the origin site of the process. If the response indicates that the process is on a different site, the message is repeated to that site.

SIGGRP (*Need-small-response*) Deliver a signal to a process group. In order to guarantee delivery of the signal to all processes in the process group, this message is sent first to the origin site of the process group and the origin site, prohibits all processes from moving, and then sends this message to all sites which have members of the specified process group.

SIGUID (*Need-small-response*) This message is broadcast to all sites to deliver a signal to all processes of a particular user id.

GSPGRP (*Need-small-response*) Get or set the process group of a process. If the site on which a process is executing isn't known, this message is first sent to the origin site of the process. If the response indicates that the process is on another site, the message is repeated to that site.

INFERIOR (child -> parent; *Need-small-response*) This message is sent from a process's site to its parent's site to find out if the first process is a descendant of a specified process. This information is used to determine if a signal should be delivered to a process of a user id different from the signaler.

The next set of messages are for Remote Character Devices:

RCDW (US -> SS; *Need-small-response*) Remote Character Device Write; sent with up to approximately 80 bytes of data to be queued for the terminal; the response indicates whether the data can be taken immediately; if the data cannot be taken immediately, the kernel process servicing the request doesn't exit, but waits for the data to be taken and then sends an RC_RWDLY message to the US.

RCDR (US -> SS; *Need-small-response*) Remote Character Device Read; request some bytes from the terminal; if data is immediately available, up to approximately 80 bytes of it is sent back in the response; if no data is available, the kernel process doesn't exit after sending the response, but instead waits for the data to arrive and then sends an RC_RWDLY message to the US.

RC_RWDLY (SS -> US; *Serviced-by-interrupt*) Delayed response to RCDR or RCDW message. If the response to a RCDW or RCDR message indicated that the data transfer could not be completed immediately, this message is later sent when that transfer does complete.

RCDIO (US -> SS; *Need-small-response*) Remote Character Device IOCTL; request to change terminal modes; the response indicates if the request can be processed immediately; if not, the kernel processes servicing the request doesn't exit, but instead waits for the request to be processed and then sends an RC_IODLY message to the US.

RD_IODLY (SS -> US; *Serviced-by-interrupt*) Delayed response to RCDIO message. If the response to an RCDIO message indicated that the operation could not be completed immediately, this message is later sent when the requested change to terminal modes has been completed.

RCDCAN (US -> SS) Cancel a Remote Character Device request. This message is sent when a process waiting for an RC_RWDLY or RC_IODLY message receives a signal and needs to cancel a remote character device operation.

The next set of messages have to do with globally mounting and unmounting filesystems. They are sent during the course of normal operations and are not confined to reconciliation and reconfiguration activities.

MTNOTIF (US -> all; *Need-small-response*) Tell the world you are mounting a given filesystem on a given file; loop through each site that is up; if any complain, call reconfiguration since then some sites will think it is mounted and others won't; information sent is gfs and pack number being mounted and <gfs,inode> that is being mounted on.

OKTOUMT (US -> all; *Need-small-response*) Ask all sites if it is ok to unmount a given pack of a filegroup (gfs). If any indicates that it is busy, fail. If any site indicates that it also has a pack of that filegroup mounted, some limited reconciliation is needed.

UMTNOTIF (US -> all; *Need-small-response*) Actual unmount notification; again sent from the requesting site to all sites; if any respond with a complaint, network reconfiguration should be called.

The next set of messages are for network reconfiguration.

CHNOPN (*Special*) Sent as the first message from one site to a site which it believes was or is down. Contained in this message is a unique channel number which is used for further communications, thereby eliminating any old messages that may still be in transit from an earlier connection with that site.

PROBE (*Large, Need-large-response, Special*) Sent from one site to another to find out if it is still up. A page of data and checksum is sent in both the message and response to verify the integrity of the communication channel.

SITEDOWN (*Need-small-response, Special*) Sent from a site when it believes some other site has gone down; sent in order of lowest site first; if the responder is a lower numbered site, the originator stops sending SITEDOWN and the responder site continues.

NEWPARTSET (*Special*) Broadcast (site by site) from the lowest numbered site in the partition to all other sites in the partition telling them who is in the partition.

GETTOP (*Special*) Asynchronous request sent from the lowest numbered site in the partition to all other sites in a partition requesting information about filegroups that are mounted at those sites. Asynchronous response is PMOUNT.

PMOUNT (*Large, Special*) Asynchronous response to GETTOP, sent by each member of a partition to the site running the reconfiguration (the lowest numbered site in the partition). This message contains information about each of the filegroups mounted locally.

NEWTOP (*Large, Special*) Broadcast (site by site) from the reconfiguration site to all members of a partition, telling them all the information about all the mounted filesystems.

SNDIND (CSS -> SS; *Need-large-response, Special*) Sent from a CSS to each site which stores a copy of a filegroup, requesting a list of which files in the filegroup are open.

Interprocess Communication messages:

IPCLOOKUP (*Need-small-response*) Sent from user to IPCNS to look up a given key. A flag, also passed in this message, may specify the key and associated object be allocated if not found. A handle is returned.

IPCHANDLE (*Need-small-response*) An IPCLOOKUP may require a handle be allocated. This message is sent to the storge site to allocate the handle. The response returns a handle.

MSGSTAT (*Need-large-response*) This message is sent to the storage site to request status information about a queue. The buffer returns request information.

MSGSET (*Large, Need-small-response*) Sent to the storage site to set a queue's status information. The response indicates if an error arose.

MSGSEND (*Large, Need-small-response*) Transfers a System V IPC message from the using site to the queue at the storage site. Since System V IPC messages can be larger than the current /*L system buffer size, more than one of these messages may be sent to effect the transfer.

MSGRECEIVE (*Need-large-response*) Transfer a System V IPC message from the queue at the storage site to the user. The initial request causes portions of the IPC message to be transferred until the entire message has been received at the using site.

MSGRMID (*Need-small-response*) Sent to remove a queue from a storage site.

IPCNSRMID (*Need-small-response*) Sent from the storage site to the IPCNS site. It removes the key associated with the queue in the IPCNS database.

SEMCTL1 (*Need-small-response*) Used for all semaphore operations that require a small response. Subtype field indicates actual semaphore operation.

SEMCTL2 (*Large, Need-large-response*) Used for all semaphore operations that require a large response. Subtype field indicates actual semaphore operation.

SEMOPS (*Large, Need-small-response*) Sent to the storage site to initiate semaphore operations specified in the buffer sent. The update is performed at the storage site atomically.

SEMSLPCAN () Sent from a semaphore process who was instructed to sleep to notify another process that it has been interrupted. For semaphores, those sleeping on the semaphore are awoken if necessary. SEMAOE () Sent to storage site from using site to adjust semphore values on process exit.

Miscellaneous messages:

ACK (*Special*) Message acknowledgement, currently sent in response to almost all other messages, including response messages. Basically a lower level message.

DEBUG () Remote control message for debugging. This message allows one site to request another site to print some of its kernel data structures on its operator's console or to take a core dump and reboot.

TIMESYNC () This message is sent from one site to another to calibrate the clocks so that the clocks on all sites in the network are kept in agreement.

WAKEUP () This message is sent from one site to another to wake up a process if a previous message instructed that process to sleep.

SLPCAN () This message is sent from a process who was instructed to sleep to notify another process that it has been interrupted and is no longer sleeping.

Bibliography

In the following references, *ACM* stands for Association for Computing Machinery, *CACM* stands for *Communications of the Association For Computing Machinery, IEEE* stands for *Institute of Electronic and Electrical Engineers,* and *SOSP* stands for *Symposium on Operating System Principles and COMPCON stands for* IEEE Computer Society International Conference..

Abr 63	Abramson, N., *Information Theory and Coding,* McGraw-Hill, New York, N.Y., 1963.
And 83	Andrews, R., *Maintaining Network Transparency over Slow Links,* Masters Thesis, UCLA Computer Science, 1983.
Als 76	Alsberg, P. A., Day, J. D., *A Principle for Resilient Sharing of Distributed Resources,* Second International Conference on Software Engineering, San Francisco, California, October 13-15, 1976, pp. 562-570.
Ant 80	Antonelli, Hamilton, et al., *SDS/NET - An Interactive Distributed OS,* Proceedings COMPCON Fall 1980.
Bar 81	Bartlett J.F., *A NonStop Kernel,* Proceedings of the Eighth SOSP, Pacific Grove, California, December 1981, pp. 22-29.
Ber 80	Bernstein, P., *Algorithms for Concurrency Control in Distributed Database Systems,* Technical Report CCA-80-05, Computer Corporation of America, February 1980.
Bir 82	Birrell, A. D., Levin, R., Needham, R. M., Schroeder, M. D., *Grapevine: An Exercise in Distributed Computing,* CACM, Vol. 25, No. 4, April 1982, pp. 260-274.
Bro 82	Brownbridge, D., L. Marshall, B. Randell, *The Newcastle Connection,* Software- Practice and Experience, Vol. 12, pp. 1147-1162, 1982.
Che 79	Cheriton D.C., M.A. Malcolm, L.S. Melen, and G.R. Sager, *Thoth, a portable real-time operating system.* CACM 22(2):105-115, February 1979.
Che 83	Cheriton, D., *Local Networking and Internetworking in the V System,* Proceedings of the 8th Data Communications Symposium, North Falmouth, MA., pp. 9-16, Oct. 1983.

Cla 78   Clark, D., K. Pogran, and D. Reed, *An Introduction to Local Area Networks*, Proceedings of the IEEE, Vol. 66, No. 11, November, 1978, pp. 1497-1517.

Cla 80   Clark, D., Svobodova, L., *Design of Distributed Systems Supporting Local Autonomy*, Proceedings COMPCON, Feb. 1980.

Coh 81   Cohen, D., *On Holy Wars and a Plea for Peace*, IEEE Computer, October 1981, pp. 48-54.

Dar 81   *DARPA Internet Protocol and Internet Control Message Protocol Specification*, RFC 791, 792, USC/Information Sciences Institute, Los Angeles, CA., Sept. 1981.

Dec 81   Digitial Equipment Corporation, Software Product Description, DECnet-VAX, Version 2.0, VAX/VMS Network Software.

Den 72   Denning, P., *On Modeling Program Behavior*, Proceedings Spring Joint Computer Conference, vol. 40, AFIPS Press, 1972, pp. 937-944.

Dio 80   Dion, J., *The Cambridge File Server*, Operating Systems Review 14(4), pp. 26-35, Oct. 1980.

DoD 80   *DoD Standard Internet Protocol*, ACM Computer Communication Review, Vol. 10, No. 4, Oct. 1980.

Dow 80   Dowdy, L., Foster, D., *Comparative Models of the File Assignment Problem*, Computing Surveys, Vol. 14, No. 2, June 1982, pp. 287-313.

Edw 82   Edwards, D. A., *Implementation of Replication in LOCUS: A Highly Reliable Distributed Operating System*, Masters Thesis, Computer Science Department, University of California, Los Angeles, 1982.

Fai 81   Faissol, S., *Availability and Reliability Issues in Distributed Databases*, PhD. Dissertation, Computer Science Department, University of California, Los Angeles, 1981.

For 78   Forsdick, Schantz, Thomas, *Operating Systems for Computer Networks*, IEEE Computer, Jan. 1978.

Fri 81   Fridrich, M., W. Older, *The FELIX File Server*, Proceedings of the Eighth SOSP, Pacific Grove, California, December 1981, pp. 37-44.

Gal 78   Gallager,R., *Variations on a Theme by Huffman*, IEEE Transactions on Information Theory, Vol. IT-24, No. 6, Nov. 1978.

Gel 77   Geller D.P., *The National Software Works -- Access to distributed files and tools*, Proceedings National Conference 53-58 ACM, October 1977.

Gra 78   Gray, J. N., *Notes on Data Base Operating Systems*, Operating Systems, Lecture Notes in Computer Science 60, Springer-Verlag, 1978, 393-481.

Han 84   Hanson, S., Kraut, R., and Farber, J, *Interface Design and Multivariate Analysis of Unix Command Use*, ACM Transactions on Office Information Systems, Vol. 2, No. 1, January, 1984.

Hin 83   Hinden, R., Haverty, J., Sheltzer, A., *The DARPA Internet: Interconnecting Heterogeneous Computer Networks with Gateways*, IEEE Computer, Sept., 1983

Hol 81a   Holler E., *Multiple Copy Update*, Distributed Systems - Architecture and Implementation, Lecture Notes in Computer Science 105, Springer-Verlag, 1981, 284-303.

Hol 81b   Holler E., *The National Software Works (NSW)*, Distributed Systems - Architecture and Implementation, Lecture Notes in Computer Science 105, Springer-Verlag, 1981, 421-442.

Hwa 82   Hwang, et. al. *A Unix-Based Local Computer Network with Load Balancing*, IEEE Computer, April 1982.

Isr 83   Israel and Linden, *Authentication in Office System Internetworks*, ACM Transactions on Office Information Systems, July 1983.

Kea 83   Kearns, DeFazio, *Locality of Reference in Hierarchical Database Systems*, IEEE Transactions on Software Engineering, March 1983.

Kle 75   Kleinrock, L., Opderbeck, H., *Throughput in the Arpanet - Protocols and Measurement* Fourth Data Communications Symposium, Quebec City, Canada, October 7-9 , 1975, pp. 6-1 to 6-11.

Lam 81a   Lampson B.W., *Atomic Transactions*, Distributed Systems - Architecture and Implementation, Lecture Notes in Computer Science 105, Springer-Verlag, 1981, 246-264.

Lam 81b   Lampson B.W., *Ethernet, Pub and Violet*, Distributed Systems Architecture and Implementation, Lecture Notes in Computer Science 105, Springer-Verlag, 1981, 446-484.

Lam 79   Lampson, B.W. and H.E. Sturgis, *Crash Recovery in a Distributed Data Storage System*, (a Working Paper), Xerox Palo Alto Research Center, April 29, 1979.

Lan 80   Lantz K.A., *Uniform Interfaces for Distributed Systems*, PhD. Dissertation, Computer Science Department, University of Rochester, May 1980.

Laz 84   Lazowska, E., J. Zahorjan, D. Cheriton, W. Zwaenepoel, *File Access Performance of Diskless Workstations*, Stanford University Technical Report 84-06-01, June 1984.

Lea 82   Leach, P.J., B.L. Stumpf, J.A. Hamilton, and P.H. Levine, *UIDs as Internal Names in a Distributed File System*, ACM Sigact-Sigops Symposium on Principles of Distributed Computing, Ottawa, Canada, August 18-20, 1982.

LeB 82   LeBlanc, T. J., *The Design and Performance of High-Level Language Primitives for Distributed Programming*, PhD. Dissertation, Computer Sciences Department, University of Wisconsin-Madison, December 1982. Also Computer Sciences Technical Report #492.

Lel 81   LeLann G., *Synchronization*, Distributed Systems - Architecture and Implementation, Lecture Notes in Computer Science 105, Springer-Verlag, 1981, 266-282.

Lin 79   Lindsay, B. G. et. al., *Notes on Distributed Databases*, IBM Research Report RJ2571(33471), IBM Research Laboratory, San Jose, CA, July 14, 1979, 44-50.

Lin 80a   Lindsay, B.G., *Object Naming and Catalog Management for a Distributed Database Manager*, IBM Research Report RJ2914(36689), IBM Research Laboratory, San Jose, CA, August 29, 1980.

Lin 80b   Lindsay, B.G., *Site Autonomy Issues in R*; A Distributed Database Management System*, IBM Research Report RJ2927(36822), IBM Research Laboratory, San Jose, CA, September 15, 1980.

Lin 80c   Lindsay, B.G., *R* Notes from the IEEE Workshop on Fundamental Issues in Distributed Systems, Pala Mesa, California, Dec. 15-17, 1980.

Lin 84   Lindsay, B., Haas, L., Mohan, C., Wilms, F., Yost, R., *Computation and Communication in R*: A Distributed Database Manager*, ACM Transactions on Computer Systems, Vol. 2. No. 1, Feb. 1984, pp. 1-15..

Lis 82   Liskov,B., *On Linguistic Support for Distributed Programs*, IEEE Trans. on Software Eng., May 1982.

Mad 76   Madison, A., Batson, A., *Characteristics of Program Localities*, CACM, Vol. 19, No. 5, May 1976.

Mit 82   Mitchell, J. and Dion, A., A Comparison of Two Network-Based File Servers, CACM, Vol. 25, No. 4, April 1982.

Moo 82   Moore, J. D., *Simple Nested Transactions in LOCUS: A Distributed Operating System,* Master's Thesis, Computer Science Department, University of California, Los Angeles, 1982.

Mue 83a   Mueller E., *Implementation of Nested Transactions in a Distributed System,* Master's Thesis, Computer Science Department, University of California, Los Angeles, 1983.

Mue 83b   Mueller E., J. Moore and G. Popek, *A Nested Transaction System for LOCUS,* Proceedings of the 9th ACM SOSP, Oct. 1983, pp. 71-89.

Nel 81   Nelson, B.J., *Remote Procedure Call,* PhD. Dissertation, Report CMU-CS-81-119, Carnegie-Mellon University, Pittsburgh, 1981.

Opp 83   Oppen and Dalal, *The Clearinghouse: A Decentralized Agent for Locating Names Objects in a Distributed Environment,* ACM Transactions on Office Information Systems, July 1983.

Ous 80a   Ousterhout, J.K. D.A. Scelze, and P.S. Sindhu, *Medusa: An experiment in distributed operating system design.* CACM 23(2):92-105, February 1980.

Ous 80b   Ousterhout J.K, *Partitioning and Cooperation in a Distributed Multiprocessor Operating System: Medusa.* PhD. Dissertation, Carnegie-Mellon University, April 1980.

Par 83   Parker, D. Stott, Popek, Gerald J., Rudisin, G., Stoughton, A., Walker, B., Walton, E., Chow, J., Edwards, D:, Kiser, S., and Kline, C., *Detection of Mutual Inconsistency in Distributed Systems,* IEEE Transactions of Software Engineering, May 1983, pp. 240-247.

Pop 81   Popek, G., Walker, B., Chow, J., Edwards, D., Kline, C., Rudisin, G., and Thiel, G., *LOCUS: A Network Transparent, High Reliability Distributed System,* Proceedings of the Eighth SOSP, Pacific Grove, California, December 1981, pp. 169-177.

Ras 80   Rashid R.F, *A network operating system kernel for SPICE/DSN.* Internal Memo, Computer Science Department, Carnegie-Mellon University, November 1980.

Ras 81   Rashid, R.F., and Robertson, G.G., *Accent: A Communication Oriented Network Operating System Kernel,* Proceedings of the Eighth SOSP, Pacific Grove, California, December 1981, pp. 64-75.

Ree 78   Reed, D. P., *Naming and Synchronization in a Decentralized Computer System*, Technical Report MIT/LCS/TR-205, Laboratory for Computer Science, M.I.T., 1978.

Ree 80   Reed, D.P, and Svobodova L, *SWALLOW: A Distributed Data Storage System for a Local Network*, Proceedings of the International Workshop on Local Networks, Zurich, Switzerland, August 1980.

Rit 78   Ritchie, D. and Thompson, K., *The UNIX Timesharing System*, Bell System Technical Journal, vol. 57, no. 6, part 2 (July - August 1978), 1905-1930.

Row 82   Rowe and Birman, *A local Network Based on the UNIX OS*, IEEE Transactions on Software Engineering, March 1982.

Sal 78   Saltzer J.H., *Naming and Binding of Objects*, Operating Systems, Lecture Notes in Computer Science 60, Springer-Verlag, 1978, 99-208.

Sal 80   Saltzer, J., D. Reed, and D. Clark, *End-to-End Arguments in System Design*, Notes from IEEE Workshop on Fundamental Issues in Distributed Systems, Pala Mesa, California, Dec 15-17, 1980.

She 85   Sheltzer, A. *Network Transparency in an Internetwork Environment*, Ph.D. Dissertation, Computer Science Department, University of California, Los Angeles, 1985.

Spe 82   Spector, A. Z., *Performing Remote Operations Efficiently on a Local Computer Network*, CACM, Vol. 25, No. 4, April 1982.

Sto 76   Stonebraker, M., and E. Neuhold, *A Distributed Database Version of INGRES*, Electronics Research Laboratory, College of Engineering, University of California, Berkeley, Memo No. ERL-M612, September 11, 1976.

Stu 80   Sturgis, H.E. J.G, Mitchell and J. Israel, *Issues in the Design and Use of a Distributed File System*, Operating Systems Review 14(3), pp. 55-69, July 1980.

Svo 81   Svobodova, L., *A Reliable Object-Oriented Data Repository For a Distributed Computer*, Proceedings of the Eighth SOSP, Pacific Grove, California, December 1981, pp. 47-58.

Tan 81   Tanenbaum,A., *Computer Networks*, Prentice-Hall, Englewood Cliffs, New Jersey, 1981.

146

Thi 83   Thiel, G., *Partitioned Operation and Distributed Data Base Management System Catalogs*, PhD. Dissertation, Computer Science Department, University of California, Los Angeles, 1983.

Tho 73   Thomas R.H, *A Resource Sharing Executive for the ARPANET*. Proceedings National Computer Conference 42:155-163, AFIPS, June 1973.

Tho 78   Thomas, R.F., *A Solution to the Concurrency Control Problem for Multiple Copy Data Bases*, Proceedings Spring COMPCON, Feb 28-Mar 3, 1978.

Tho 79   Thomas R.H., *A Majority Consensus Approach to Concurrency Control for Multiple Copy Databases*, ACM Transactions of Database Systems 4(2), June 1979.

Tsa 83   Tsay, Liu, *MIKE. A Network Operating System for the Distributed Double-Loop Computer Network*, IEEE Transactions on Software Eng., March 1983.

Wal 83a   Walker, B., *Issues of Network Transparency and File Replication in the Distributed Filesystem Component of LOCUS*, Ph.D. Dissertation, UCLA Computer Science, 1983.

Wal 83b   Walker,B., Popek, G., English, B., Kline, C., Thiel, G., *The LOCUS Distributed Operating System*, Proceedings of the 9th ACM Symposium on Operating System Principles, Oct., 1983. pp. 49-70

Wat 81   Watson R.W., *Identifiers (Naming) in Distributed Systems*, Distributed Systems - Architecture and Implementation, Lecture Notes in Computer Science 105, Springer-Verlag, 1981, 191-210.

Wil 80   Wilkes, M., and R. Needham, *The Cambridge Model Distributed System*, Notes from IEEE Workshop on Fundamental Issues in Distributed Systems, Pala Mesa, California, Dec 15-17, 1980.

Xer 80   Xerox, *The Ethernet: A Local Area Network - Data Link Layer and Physical Layer Specifications, Version 1.0*, Sept 30, 1980. Available from Digital Equipment Corporation, Maynard, Massachusetts; Intel Corporation, Santa Clara, California; Xerox Corporation, Stamford, Connecticut.

Index

Network transparency 1, 7
New partition set 93
Nomad 118
Offset token 53
Operating system heterogeneity 19
Optimization language 12
Origin site 84
OSITE 84
PGRPs 75
PID 75
Pack number 36
Page swapping 83
Partial failure 22
Partition protocol 93
Partition set 93
Partitioned operation 62
Pathname searching 45
Performance requirements 3
Pipe 58
Primary copy 36
Primary pack 37, 62
Primary site 62
Problem-oriented protocols 67
Process family 52
Process group 52, 75
Process group tracking 85
Process identifier 75
Process naming 75
Process tracking 84
Propagation (of file updates) 48
Protection 24
Pulling protocol 77, 78
RS 59
Reading site 59
Remote devices 70
Remote tasking 73

Replication 35
Run 74
SS 59
Semantic consistency 9
Server processes 32
Setpath 103
Setxperm 82
Setxsites 74, 82
Shadow page 47
Sigmigrate 74
Signals 89
Signet daemon 89
Site identifier 75
SID 75
Storage site 41, 59
Surrogate origin site 84
Synchronization 41
System configuration 105
Token manager site 53, 54
Tokens 52, 53, 54, 55
Transparency 1, 6, 7, 9, 23
Unbuffered devices 72
Unix compatibility 3
Using site 41
WS 59
Water-mark 63
Workstation topology 108
Writing site 59

Printed in the United States
By Bookmasters